The Christian's Promised Land

Studies in Joshua

J. OSWALD SANDERS

KINGSWAY PUBLICATIONS
EASTBOURNE

ISBN 0 86065 266 1

Unless otherwise indicated, Scripture quotations
are from the New International Version, © New York
International Bible Society 1978

Printed in Great Britain for
KINGSWAY PUBLICATIONS LTD
Lottbridge Drove, Eastbourne, E. Sussex BN23 6NT by
Richard Clay (The Chaucer Press) Ltd, Bungay, Suffolk.
Typeset by Nuprint Services Ltd, Harpenden, Herts.

CONTENTS

PREFACE

The material in this book has been used by the author in a series of messages, and some portions have appeared in written form not now in print.

It does not purport to be an exposition of the Book of Joshua, although it does cover the main features of that book. In the writer's opinion, no book in the Old Testament is more helpful in teaching lessons of spiritual relevance to the Christian life.

One writer has justifiably observed that some preachers and expositors have obscured the text of the Book through excessive spiritualization and typology, and this tends to make it more difficult to understand the Book.

I have endeavoured to preserve a balance in this respect. In an introductory note I advance a New Testament warrant and precedent for drawing spiritual lessons from certain historical events. The very real moral problem raised by the divine command to totally destroy the nations of Canaan is faced realistically.

The Book of Joshua, interpreted in the light of

Ephesians and Hebrews, presents an optimistic prospect for the Christian who purposes to have God's best in his spiritual life. It also reveals with painful clarity the pitfalls he is liable to encounter.

If some readers are encouraged to take the step of faith that leaves behind the frustrations of the desert-life and enters upon the rest and victory of the Canaan-life, the purpose of the book will be achieved.

J. Oswald Sanders

INTRODUCTORY NOTE

Certain passages in the New Testament appear to indicate that the epic trek of the Israelites from Egypt, through the Sinai desert into Canaan, and their subsequent subjugation of that land, are of more than mere historical value. References to those events by Paul and the writer of the Letter to the Hebrews, seem to confirm that this was the intention of the inspiring Spirit. They have no hesitation in drawing spiritual lessons from selected historical incidents in the Old Testament.

Twice Paul asserts that the history of Israel is typical history that has spiritual relevance for Christians in this age:

Now these things occurred as examples, to keep us from setting our hearts on evil things as they did... (1 Cor 10:6).

These things happened to them as examples, and *were written down as warnings for us*, on whom the fulfilment of the ages has come (1 Cor 10:11, italics mine).

9

The word 'examples' comes from the Greek *tupoi* which can mean either 'an example', as in 1 Timothy 4:12, or 'a type of a fact or spiritual truth'. Marvin Vincent says that the best texts of the latter verse read 'by way of figure'.

The writer to the Hebrews also draws contemporary spiritual lessons from Israel's experiences:

Who were they who heard and rebelled? Were they not all those Moses led out of Egypt? And with whom was he angry for forty years? Was it not with those who sinned, whose bodies fell in the desert? And to whom did God swear that they would never enter his rest if not to those who disobeyed?

Let us be careful that none of you be found to have fallen short of it (Heb 3:16–18; 4:1).

So while undue spiritualizing of Old Testament incidents is to be avoided, here and elsewhere we have Scriptural authorization and precedent for drawing spiritual lessons from these historical events.

It is rightly observed by George Turner that allegory is often carried too far by enthusiastic preachers and expositors, for it easily lends itself to fanciful and irresponsible imagination. But used with discretion it can be helpful.[1]

In the *Westminster Commentary*, H. L. Goudge says in this connection:

We can hardly doubt that Paul regarded these Old Testament incidents as not merely valuable illustrations, but as pre-arranged types of Christian mysteries. Such views may appear fanciful to the modern mind, but deeper knowledge of the Scriptures will probably convince of their truth....

If God's dealings with Israel had a special purpose which his dealings with other nations had not, a true narrative of these dealings will of necessity have a special didactic character.

While the context varies from age to age, the great spiritual principles underlying God's dealings with His people do not vary greatly. In every age there are similar causes of failure and declension, and, thankfully, similar conditions of progress and victory. In both Old and New Testaments there are preserved for posterity wonderful examples of faith and courage, and also strong warnings against unbelief and apostasy (both corporate and personal).

THE PREPARATION OF A LEADER

Under Moses, Joshua learned to serve. This was a necessary part of his training. God knew Joshua better than he knew himself or anyone else knew him, so He put him under discipline to Moses and compelled the mettlesome and impatient servant to obey commands and execute orders. It was not until he had spent what seemed the better part of a lifetime taking orders that he was set in a place of command and permitted to issue them.

Some persons are said to be natural leaders, and this often means nothing more than that they are by nature dictatorial and overbearing, enjoying nothing so much as 'lording it over God's heritage'. God understands the strength and the weakness of such persons and prepares them for usefulness by putting them in the school of obedience. Joshua was such a man. Moses himself had led sheep before he was qualified to lead Israel, and Joshua had to learn to obey Moses before he would be fit to command Israel.

A. W. Tozer

Through men whom worldlings count as fools,
    Chosen of God and not of man,
Reared in Thy secret training schools,
    Moves forward Thine eternal plan.

And now, though hidden from our ken
    In Midian desert, Sinai's hill,
Spirit of God Thou has Thy men
    Waiting Thy time to do Thy will.

When blazing out upon our night
    Flashes the Pentecostal flame,
May I be found with heart alight,
    Burning to magnify Thy name.

Not as the prophets who declare
    The Word that thousands hear and own,
If I may have the smallest share
    In setting Christ upon His throne

Frank Houghton

Chapter 1

THE PREPARATION OF A LEADER

Joshua, the son of Nun, walked on to the pages of history at a crucial moment in the life of the Hebrew nation. This man, chosen by God to lead Israel out of the desert and into the Land of Promise, was born in Egyptian slavery about 1500 B.C. Whether he personally experienced the sting of the taskmaster's lash is not recorded, but he doubtless experienced most of the frustrations and limitations of a slave's lot.

From the time of the Exodus (*c.* 1446 BC), his name is prominent and intimately linked with the fortunes of his nation. His achievements won for him an honoured place among Israel's famous leaders. General O. O. Howard paid him this tribute:

> As regards his genius for military leadership, he had a great natural talent for organization, for planning and the strategic conduct of a campaign; for fighting a battle and keeping the love and confidence of his soldiers, and with confidence in his own cause, never forgetting to lean on the arm of his Lord in defeat or victory.[2]

A discerning spiritual leader such as Moses would be both careful and prayerful in his selection of an aide.

Joshua's subsequent career fully vindicated his choice.

He lacks the great peaks of character which distinguish his leader, Moses. But this brings him nearer to our own level and constitutes him a type of the faithful, consistent man who God can use in his truceless warfare against the forces of evil.

When Joshua appears abruptly on the page of Scripture and history, it is in the role he was later to fill with such distinction: a soldier – leader.

No sooner had the Israelites arrived at Rephidim, than they were subjected to a ruthless and unprovoked attack by the Amalekites, a nomadic, marauding people who lived in the Negev. The relevant Scriptures make it clear that the attack was not only cowardly, but was consciously directed against Israel's God. This attitude characterized the Amalekites throughout their history.

Moses said, 'For *hands were lifted up to the throne of the Lord*. The Lord will be at war with Amalek from generation to generation' (Ex 17:16, italics mine). The Lord said to Moses, 'Write this on a scroll as something to be remembered and make sure that Joshua hears it, because I will completely erase the memory of Amalek from under heaven' (Ex 17:14).

Moses later recalls this incident, and charges Israel to be the executors of His judgement. God will never tolerate rebellion, and He will judge wanton cruelty.

Remember what the Amalekites did to you along the way when you came out of Egypt. When you were weary and worn out, they met you on your journey and cut off all who were lagging behind; *they had no fear of God*.

When the Lord your God gives you rest from all the enemies around you in the land he is giving you to possess as an inheritance, you shall blot out the memory of Amalek from under heaven. Do not forget! (Deut 25:17–19, italics mine).

A significant sequel occurred in the life of King Saul who was charged to utterly destroy the Amalekites for the manner in which they waylaid Israel. He obediently attacked them but he 'took Agag king of the Amalekites alive....Saul...spared Agag' (1 Sam 15:7–9). It was at the hand of an Amalekite that Saul met his own death! (2 Sam 4:1–10).

The battle at Rephidim (Ex 17:8–16) marked an important step in the training and equipment of the man whom God had chosen to lead His people to victory in the Land of Promise. There he learned two valuable lessons—that prayer is mightier than the sword, and that God was committed to the protection and defence of His people. He would not leave unpunished those who defied Him and wantonly molested His people. These lessons were to prove of great value to Joshua in the long campaign that lay ahead.

Between two cryptic sentences: 'The Amalekites came and attacked the Israelites', and 'Joshua overcame the Amalekite army', stands a third, 'I will stand on the top of the hill with the staff of God in my hands' (Ex 17:8, 9, 13). The last statement was the fulcrum on which victory turned.

This pictorial representation of God's strategy for victory in spiritual warfare is aptly expressed by the poet William Cowper:

Restraining prayer, we cease to fight,
Prayer keeps the Christian's armour bright,
And Satan trembles when he sees
The weakest saint upon his knees.

While Moses stood with arms spread wide,
Success was found on Israel's side;
But when through weariness they failed,
That moment Amalek prevailed.

Moses entrusted the leadership of the army to his young aide, Joshua, while he, with staff in hand and accompanied by Aaron and Hur, made his way to the top of a hill overlooking the battleground. To Moses, the rod which he had stretched out over the Red Sea not long before was 'the staff of God', and it was to play a significant part in this battle. It was not an instrument of magic, but it represented the power and authority of God which He had delegated to his servant (Ex 4:1–4).

Two groups were engaged in this conflict with the enemy, isolated from each other, and yet inextricably linked: three unarmed octogenarians inactive on the hilltop, and Joshua and his army struggling in battle in the valley. The chosen leader's function was to hold up the staff of God, the chosen soldiers', to engage in hand-to-hand battle with the enemy. Each had a distinctive function and each would have failed had the roles been reversed. In the fluctuation of the battle, the key to victory was in the hands of the intercessors on the hill. The weaponless hands of prayer controlled the tides of battle.

When Moses' arms grew weary with holding up the

staff of God by means of which he visibly asserted the authority and power of God over the foe, his two friends 'held his hands up...so that his hands remained steady until sunset' (Ex 17:12). The seeming inactivity on the hill required as great a stamina as the activity in the valley. So long as Moses exercised his delegated authority, Amalek was kept on the run.

> Faith is an affirmation and an act
> That makes eternal truth be fact.

It was neither Moses, nor the staff, but God who won the battle. Joshua had to fight as if there were no uplifted staff. Moses must hold the staff aloft as though there were no drawn sword. Which is an allegory.

The uplifted staff indicated the presence of a third force on the field, and of this Joshua was soon to learn more.

It was later the young man's privilege to be present at the tent of meeting, when 'the Lord would speak to Moses face to face, as a man speaks with his friend' (Ex 33:11), and it is recorded of him that when Moses returned to the camp, 'his young assistant Joshua did not leave the tent'. He delighted to be in the place where God manifested his presence. He also accompanied his leader to that memorable meeting on Mount Sinai, and shared, although at a distance, those awe-filled meetings of Moses with his God. Such experiences are transforming for one can never see the majesty and glory of God and be the same again.

Isaac Stern, the famous musician, once said that of all the instruments in the orchestra the second fiddle was the most difficult to master. But in this role Joshua displayed great virtuosity. He began his career as second to Moses and, as we shall see later, he had no sooner been commissioned to succeed him, than he was charged to surrender his command and become second to the new Commander-in-chief of the Lord's army.

Not every one has the stature to accept demotion cheerfully. But Joshua would sooner be second-in-command of the Lord's army than commander-in-chief of his own. Few Christian leaders pass this test with flying colours.

> The heights by great men reached and kept
>   Were not attained in sudden flight,
> But they while their companions slept
>   Were toiling upwards in the night.
>
> Standing on what too long we bore,
>   With shoulders bent and downcast eyes,
> We may discern—unseen before—
>   A path to higher destinies.
>
> *Longfellow*

While God's strategy varies from age to age, the preparation of the man of God remains substantially the same. Joshua's apprenticeship under Moses afforded him a unique training, not least in the knowledge of God.

The divine intervention at the Red Sea, the provision in the desert, the miraculous guidance through the pillar of cloud and fire, would all deeply affect the young man's impressionable heart and develop in him a deepening sense of confidence in God. He learned that there is everything in God to be trusted, but he had also witnessed His strange work of judgement and realized that there is also in God something to be feared.

Few leaders have had their commissioning service conducted by God, as Joshua did (Josh 1:1–9). In it He enunciated the unchanging principles for prosperity and success in His service. The call to Joshua was crystal clear and the terms of his commission plainly defined.

It is significant that on the death of Moses God did not appoint the Committee of Seventy, who had assisted him in administration, to lead the nation. He chose a man whom He had prepared and who He saw possessed the natural and spiritual qualifications for the monumental task.

As a leader, Joshua demonstrated the power of *clear decision* in things of the Spirit as well as in the arts of war. Whenever the path of duty was plain to him, there was no hesitation or vacillation in his obedience. A man of decision himself, he called on others to be the same. 'Choose for yourselves this day whom you will serve' was his challenge to the nation, 'whether the gods your forefathers served beyond the River, or the gods of the Amorites in whose land you are living. But as for me and my household, we will serve the Lord' (Josh 24:15). In the contest between Jehovah and the gods of Canaan, he knew there could be no benevolent neutrality.

Many a leader has won the war but lost the peace. Perhaps Winston Churchill was one of the most unfortunate in this respect. But Joshua learned and practised the art of *true diplomacy*—the ability to reconcile conflicting viewpoints without compromising principle. His skill in this art was manifest in his conduct of the difficult and delicate task of dividing the land among the people after it had been subdued. To achieve this successfully in the face of human cupidity and covetousness required more than natural tact and wisdom. His resolution of the potentially explosive misunderstanding between Reuben and God and the other tribes, was a masterpiece of wise diplomacy—the outcome, without a doubt, of frequent communion and intimacy with God.

The quality of the leadership of this sincere and godly man appears in his closing address to the nation in which he extols the faithfulness of God.

> Now I am about to go the way of all the earth. You know with all your heart and soul that not one of all the good promises the Lord your God gave you has failed. Every promise has been fulfilled; not one has failed (Josh 23:14).

Clarence E. Macartney pays a fine tribute to this great man and leader:

> One of the noblest things about this titanic man is his noble thought for tomorrow, his desire for the generation that was to follow him.... When he realized that his own race was nearly run, and that he had fought his last battle, he called for the leaders of the people and exhorted them to hold fast to their faith in God. The approaching sunset of his own life in no respect diminished his faith or his zeal for God. 'Cleave unto the Lord your God', he said, 'for the Lord your God he it is that fighteth for you, as he hath promised you' (23:8, 11).
> To plan for the future, to think of those who come after us...this is always the mark of the highest faith and the noblest courage.[3]

A PERPLEXING MORAL PROBLEM

Genesis 14:13–16; Deuteronomy 18:10–12; 20:16–18

The destruction of the Canaanites was, like the Flood, a personal judgment by Jehovah Himself, but in this case it was executed by the agency of His chosen people at His direct command, to prepare His way for blessing on that nation, and on the whole world. They were the appointed executioners of the decree of 'the Judge of all the earth', who cannot do other than right.

Those who criticize His method, undertake a grave responsibility: for no other interpretation of the narrative itself is possible; and we must not give any quarter to modernistic ideas about the narrative. If the Israelites had obeyed implicitly, would not an indelible impression have been made on their nation with regard to the purpose of their calling, and also with reference to the abominable nature of idolatry and other sins, in the sight of God? How do we know that such a lesson could be taught so well in any other way? And they did not learn it.[4]

W. S. Hooton

With mercy and with judgment
My web of time He wove,
And aye the dews of sorrow
Were lustred by His love.

I'll bless the hand that guided,
   I'll bless the heart that planned
Where throned where glory dwelleth,
   In Immanuel's Land.

Anne Ross Cousins

Chapter 2

A PERPLEXING MORAL PROBLEM

God's gift to the nation of Israel of the land of Palestine carried with it the clear and unequivocal command that they should expel the seven Canaanite nations dwelling there—Canaanites, Hivites, Hittites, Perizzites, Gergashites, Amorites and Jebusites. If they would not depart voluntarily, they were to be utterly destroyed. Their instructions were specific:

> In the cities of the nations the Lord your God is giving you as an inheritance, do not leave alive anything that breathes. Completely destroy them...as the Lord your God has commanded you. Otherwise they will teach you all the detestable things they do in worshipping their gods, and you will sin against the Lord (Deut 20:16–18).

The demand seems harsh and uncompromising, but a reading of the history of those days reveals that wars were merciless and ruthless. Judged by the methods adopted by supposedly civilized nations in warfare in our own day—napalm, poison gas, nuclear bombs—they were very tame and small-scale affairs. However, that God would make such a demand of his people creates a deep moral problem for the thoughtful

24

reader of the Pentateuch and we must address ourselves to it.

The problem of reconciling such a command with the concept of a God of love is not easily surmounted. Was He being unjust and cruel to these nations, or were there reasons lying beneath the surface that would justify such an action?

As he faced this question and other alleged discrepancies and moral problems in the Old Testament, one Bible scholar found relief in remembering that when he was on earth our Lord faced the same difficulties and problems in His Bible. Yet He gave no indication of being disturbed by them, although they must have posed a similar problem to His sensitive nature. In fact, Deuteronomy, the Book that records this command, was one of the Lord's favourite books and the one to which He made most frequent reference.

He did not hesitate to speak freely against the errors of the religious leaders of His day, but never once did He question those portions of the Old Testament that have come under such fierce critical attack in recent years. Indeed, on the contrary, He lent His authority to the whole of the Old Testament Scriptures.

Another question has been raised. Why only the seven nations of Canaan? Were there not many other wicked nations? What was there about the Canaanites which singled them out for such condign judgement?

An important spiritual principle in God's dealings with nations is involved. Speaking to Abraham, God said:

Know for certain that your descendants will be strangers in a country not their own, and they will be enslaved and ill-treated *four hundred years*. But I will punish the nation they serve as slaves, and afterwards they will come out with great possessions…. In the fourth generation your descendants will come back here, for *the sin of the Amorites* (one of the nations of Canaan) *has not yet reached its full measure* (Gen 15:13–16, italics mine).

From this statement we learn something of the mercy and patience of God. He deals with nations according to their actions and He acts in judgement only when a nation's cup of iniquity reaches its full measure.

God made it clear to His people that His gift of Canaan was not a reward for their virtue.

Do not say to yourself, 'The Lord has brought me here to take possession of this land because of my righteousness.' No, it is on account of the wickedness of those nations that the Lord is going to drive them out before you (Deut 9:4).

Secular as well as Biblical history informs us that the nations of Canaan engaged in practices that were intolerable even to other heathen nations. Their iniquity had by then reached a point where further lenience on the part of God was impossible. They were in a position similar to that of Sodom which had become a cancerous lesion on the body of humanity. The severity of the sentence on the Canaanites only served to highlight God's implacable hostility against sin, but the divine instructions did not sanction wanton cruelty in executing the lawful sentence. Indiscriminate attack and massacre were not envisaged. Francis Schaeffer writes:

> Many of the Canaanite cities have been dug up and one can see that the statuettes which were worshipped by the Canaanites at this period were overwhelmingly perverse. The worship was wrapped up not only with complete rebellion against God, but with all kinds of sexual sin. The statuettes were as pornographic as some of today's worst pictures! And in its violence, their culture became equal to ours. So in Moses' time, God said, 'All right, it is time for the judgment'. This reminds us that there is 'death in the city' in our culture.[5]

Certain factors which throw some light on the problem should be noted.

1. The nations were given the option of making peace with Israel. 'When you march up to attack a city, make its people an offer of peace. If they accept and open their gates all the people in it shall be subject to forced labour and shall work for you' (Deut 20:10). This is what happened to the Gibeonites.

2. These nations had been granted long probation and had received many unproductive warnings. They had enjoyed the benefit of the testimony of Abraham and Melchisedec. They knew of the judgement on Sodom. With Israel on their very doorstep, they had been granted a further respite of forty years—time for repentance that went unheeded. 'God waits in long-suffering until every possibility of turning back is exhausted.'

3. The reason behind the extermination order was not military or territorial, but moral and spiritual. They were incorrigible demon-worshippers, and their moral depravity and degeneracy had reached unparalleled

depths. Had God ignored their abominations, would He not have been abdicating His responsibilities as the moral Governor of the universe?

4. One of their number, Rahab, heard God's warnings, repented and cast herself on the mercy of God. She, with the members of her family were spared. The same mercy was open to them all. Sincere repentance and turning to God was an option always open to them.

5. The extermination of the Canaanites was prophylactic in purpose—to prevent the spread of moral and spiritual infection. Since Israel was destined to fulfil such a supremely important role in God's plan for the world, He must take measures to protect them from contamination.

God's instructions to His people throw a lurid light on the demonic activities of the Canaanites:

> Let no one be found among you who sacrifices his son or daughter in the fire, who practises divination or sorcery, interprets omens, engages in witchcraft or casts spells, or who is a medium or spiritist or who consults the dead . . . *Because of these detestable practices, the Lord your God will drive out these nations before you'* (Deut 18:10–12, italics mine).

Dr Rendle Short wrote:

> It is still sound surgery to amputate the gangrenous limb. It may be harsh treatment, but it has to be done to save the life. If it is sound surgery to amputate a corrupted limb, it is only right for God to cut off a corrupted nation in the interests of society. It was as beneficent an action as the excision of a cancer in an individual.[6]

It was terrible surgery, but it was surgery, not murder. If it be asked whether some less radical action might not have sufficed, the medical answer would be that a malignancy half-treated is a malignancy untreated. By adopting these drastic measures, God gave the race a new opportunity.

6. Canaan belonged to Israel by divine gift, and so they were only taking possession of territory that was legally theirs. As Paul said in his Sermon on Mars Hill, 'He (God) fixed the epochs of their history and the limits of their territory' (Acts 17:26 NEB).

As Moses foretold, the subsequent history of Israel justified the divine action. Instead of obediently destroying the nations as they had been commanded, God's people speedily imitated their idolatry and immorality, and were themselves expelled from Canaan for their sins.

Had they obeyed, the purpose of their calling and the abhorrent nature of these sins in the sight of God would have been indelibly imprinted on their minds.

The problem of the severity of the divine judgements is not confined to the Old Testament. The New Testament declarations of judgement for impenitence and incorrigible sin are no less severe. And the most solemn warnings in this regard fell, not from the lips of Paul, but from those of the Lord of love.

The lesson for today in this act of moral surgery is that for the Christian there can be no truce in his battle with sin and the powers of evil. We must learn the lesson Israel failed to master—*no quarter must be granted to our spiritual foes*.

WHAT DOES CANAAN SYMBOLIZE?

Genesis 12:1–7; Deuteronomy 11:10–12;
Ephesians 1:13, 14

There is the Promised Land, and we can sum it up in a phrase, *the land of the life I want to live,* and the life that God's Word tells me I may live, and therefore should live—a life of victory; a life of peace, not inactivity, but peace of soul, a life of happiness and joy, though not unsympathetic with the needs of a suffering and a poor world; a life of spiritual prosperity, for I do not walk through the world without shedding a radiance about me and leaving a blessing behind me—the life that God would have me live.[7]

Colin C. Kerr

I am dwelling on the mountain
    Where the golden sunlight gleams,
O'er a land whose wondrous beauty
    Far exceeds my fondest dreams,
Where the air is pure, ethereal,
    Laden with the breath of flowers
That are blooming by the fountain
    'Neath the never fading bowers.

Is not this the Land of Beulah?
    Blessed blessed land of light

WHAT DOES CANAAN SYMBOLIZE?

Where the flowers bloom for ever,
And the sun is always bright.

Anonymous

Chapter 3

WHAT DOES CANAAN SYMBOLIZE?

The key to the spiritual interpretation and application of Israel's memorable journey and conquest lies in our understanding the significance of Canaan. What does it represent in contemporary Christian experience? The answer will be found by comparing Scripture with Scripture.

Shortly after God had called Abraham to leave his country, his people and his father's household and go to the land He would show him (Gen 12:1) and after Lot had left Abraham, God made the gift to him of Canaan, the Land of Promise. It was an astounding prospect. 'Lift up your eyes from where you are, and look north and south, east and west. All the land that you see I will give to you and your offspring for ever' (Gen 13:14, 15).

Although in the event Abraham never possessed more of the Promised Land than sufficed for a sepulchre, the gift was complete from the moment God spoke those words. Four hundred years were to elapse, however, before the promise would be realized and His people settle in Canaan.

God had led His people out of Egypt by signs and wonders, and brought them safely through the Red Sea into the Desert of Shur. From there they travelled to Kadesh-Barnea, one of the gateways into Palestine, where at last they were within sight of the Land of Promise.

Both hymnology and general usage have combined to convey the impression that the River Jordan represents physical death, and Canaan the blessedness of heaven. But only in a secondary sense is the parallel admissible. The *primary* significance of Canaan is not life in heaven, but what Paul in his Ephesian letter terms, 'life in the heavenlies'. Ephesians is the New Testament counterpart of the Book of Joshua, and throws a great deal of light upon it.

Canaan is not heaven, but a suburb of heaven. It stands for *a victorious type of Christian experience that it is possible to know and enjoy here and now*. What is presented *historically* in Joshua, is applied *spiritually* in Ephesians —the exchange of a life of defeat in the desert, for the joy, rest and fruitfulness of life in the Promised Land.

There is a Canaan rich and blest
Which all in Christ may know,
By consecrated saints possessed
While here on earth below.

There is a victory over sin,
A rest from inward strife,
A richer sense of Christ within,
A more abundant life.

J. S. Baxter

33

That Canaan cannot be identified with heaven, is clear on several counts. (a) Canaan was the scene of many battles, but there are no battles to be fought in heaven. (b) Scripture teaches that nothing that defiles can enter heaven, but Israel sinned grievously in Canaan. (c) Heaven will know no defeats, but Israel experienced defeat in Canaan. (d) In heaven there is no fear of expulsion, but the Israelites were ejected from Canaan for worshipping the gods of that nation. So we are justified in concluding that Canaan does not represent heaven, but *a life of victory attainable here and now*. It stands for a change in spiritual experience as radical and decisive as that which transformed the motley crowd of slaves into a victorious army.

The River Jordan is similarly popularly identified with *physical death*. Again, a comparison with the teaching of the New Testament shows that it can be so applied only in a secondary sense. Jordan symbolizes not physical death but the Christian's union with Christ in His death and resurrection:

> We were therefore buried with him through baptism into death in order that, just as Christ was raised from the dead through the glory of the Father, we too may live a new life. If we have been united with him in his death, we will certainly also be united with him in his resurrection (Rom 6:4, 5).

Under the charismatic leadership of Joshua, Israel left behind them the failures and frustrations of life in the barren desert and entered upon their earthly inheritance, their Land of Promise. In the parallel Ephesian Letter, Paul tells us that it is through Jesus, our heavenly Joshua, that the Christian is led out of

the barren, unsatisfying life, into his heavenly inheritance, his Promised Land, a life of fullness and satisfac-
tion (Eph. 1:13, 14).

> Living with Christ,
>   No more shall be named,
> Things of which now
>   I'm truly ashamed;
> I am from bondage
>   Utterly freed,
> Reckoning self as dead indeed.
>   Glory be to God.

T. Ryder

After the aimless years of wandering of these home-
less, stateless people, life in Canaan would have been
an alluring prospect. Through Moses, God presented
a picture so attractive that it convinced them that
Canaan held all the features of an ideal homeland.

> The Lord your God is bringing you into a good land—a
> land with streams and pools of water, with springs flow-
> ing in the valleys and hills; a land with wheat and barley,
> vines and fig-trees, pomegranates, olive oil and honey; a
> land where bread will not be scarce and you will lack
> nothing; a land where the rocks are iron and you can dig
> copper out of the hills (Deut 8:7–9).

As though further to titillate their imaginations,
God added yet more stimulating details to His des-
cription of the land, contrasting it with conditions in
Egypt after which the people were hankering:

> The land you are entering to take over is not like the land
> of Egypt, from which you have come, where you planted

35

your seed and irrigated it by foot as in a vegetable garden. But the land you are crossing the Jordan to take possession of is a land of mountains and valleys that drinks rain from heaven. It is a land your God cares for; the eyes of the Lord are continually on it from the beginning of the year to its end (Deut 11:10–12).

To the Israelites, possession of Canaan thus presented an almost irresistible option. The advantages were obvious and overwhelming:

Liberty instead of bondage

Who but a slave can appreciate the full meaning of liberty and freedom? What Canaan promised to this nation of slaves, is what God promises to the believer who is still enslaved by his sin. 'Sin shall not be your master.... You have been set free from sin and have become slaves to righteousness' (Rom 6:14, 18).

Rest instead of wandering

At long last they would have homes they could call their own. No more weary traversing the glaring sands of the desert. A similar prospect is extended to the Christian. 'There remains, then, a sabbath-rest for the people of God' (Heb 4:9). Now we who have believed, enter that rest just as God has said' (Heb 4:3).

Variety instead of monotony

In spite of their inveterate complaining and murmuring, God never allowed His people to suffer want. Never once did the manna cease or the water fail.

Their clothes did not wear out and their feet did not swell during the forty years in the desert (Deut 8:3, 4). But the monotony of their life and the sameness of their diet caused them to murmur and lust after the delicacies Egypt could supply. 'Our souls loathe this light bread,' they complained.

But Canaan offered a delightful variety of fare—milk and honey, corn and grapes and much else besides. A similar abundance and variety of spiritual fare awaits the aspiring believer in his Promised Land. When God gives, he does it magnificently: *love* that passes knowledge, *joy* unspeakable and full of glory, *peace* that passes all understanding.

Possession instead of promise

God's promise to Abraham which for centuries had remained unrealized, was at last within reach of fulfilment. The nation had only to take a daring step of faith and all this glorious prospect would become reality.

So it is for the believer who in faith steps out of the spiritual desert and enters Canaan. Promises are turned into facts, doctrine into experience. As Jesus said, according to his faith so will be his experience.

Joy instead of depression

It was God's intention that when His people entered the Promised Land, they should be a joyous people and leave the depression of the desert behind them. This is clearly stated in the provision made for their annual festivals. 'Rejoice before the Lord your God at the place he will choose as a dwelling for His name.... Be joyful at your Feast.... For the Lord your God will bless you in all your harvest and in all the work of your hands, and your joy will be complete' (Deut 16:11, 14, 15).

A similar prospect for the believer was promised by the Lord. 'I have told you this so that my joy may be in you and that your joy may be complete' (Jn 15:11).

Why do we not possess our possessions?

THE KADESH-BARNEA CRISIS

Numbers 13:17–20; 25–33; 14:1–35;
Hebrews 3:7–19; 4:1–11

Thus exaggerated and one-sided is distrust of God's promises. Such a temper is fatal to all noble life or work, and brings about the disasters which it foresees. If these cravens had gone up to fight with men before whom they felt like grasshoppers, of course they would have been beaten; and it was much better that their fears should come out at Kadesh than when committed to the struggle. Therefore God lovingly permitted the mission of the spies, and so brought lurking unbelief to the surface, where it could be dealt with.[8]

Alexander Maclaren

Kadesh-Barnea

They came to the gates of Canaan,
    But they never entered in;
They came to the very threshold,
    But they perished in their sin.

On the morrow they could have entered,
    But God had shut the gate.
They wept, they rashly ventured,
    But alas! it was too late.

And so we are ever coming
   To the place where two ways part,
One leads to the Land of Promise,
   And one to a hardened heart.

Oh, brother, give heed to the warning,
   And obey His voice today,
The Spirit to thee is calling,
   Oh do not grieve Him away.

Oh, come in complete surrender,
   Oh, turn from thy doubt and sin;
Pass on from Kadesh to Canaan
   And a crown and kingdom win.

R. Kelso Carter

Chapter 4

THE KADESH-BARNEA CRISIS

It is common in some religious circles to refer to the Christian's life on earth as a wilderness or desert experience—a bleak and unsatisfying contrast to the future life of felicity they envisage in the heavenly Canaan.

There may be some validity in the parallel, but the figure needs to be greatly qualified. Compared to our future joyous experience with our Lord in heaven, life in our tormented world may be more like a desert experience, but that is not the teaching of the projected trek from Kadesh-Barnea to Canaan, for Canaan is not heaven.

A legitimate desert experience

We must distinguish between Israel's legitimate desert experience—for they had to traverse the desert to reach the borders of Canaan—and a desert experience that was contrary to God's will. Israel, alas, experienced both.

The initial journey from the Red Sea to the Jordan

River was right and unavoidable. There is a parallel in the life of the new believer. Though redeemed by the blood of Christ and delivered from the slavery of Satan, the young Christian has yet to learn how to walk through life victoriously—through its sweet experiences, as at Elim (Ex 15:25), and its bitter experiences, as at Marah (Ex 15:23). Life in the desert was immeasurably better than the bondage of Egypt, but it fell far short of the delights of Canaan.

The nation had come to birth, but it was still in a state of spiritual infancy. The people were not yet trained and equipped for the exacting warfare that lay ahead of them in Canaan. The hardships of the desert were designed to produce this fitness. But though they were fed with 'bread from heaven', they often craved for Egypt's dainties. They sang their song of deliverance at the Red Sea (Ex 15:1–18), but ere long it died, and they were complaining at the hardness of their lot.

In the desert they were prone to lean too heavily on human props. When Moses' masterful presence was withdrawn for a brief period while he ascended Mount Sinai to meet with God, the people persuaded pliable Aaron to make a golden calf, so that they could worship it in the manner of the nations around them. They were extremely susceptible to the influence of the 'mixed multitudes' of non-Hebrews who had attached themselves to the camp. They were, in short, the counterparts of what Paul termed worldly, or carnal Christians. 'Brothers, I could not address you as spiritual, but as worldly—mere infants in Christ' (1 Cor 3:1).

In this picture, some may discern their own spiritual autobiography. Israel's desert experience on the way to Kadesh-Barnea was, however, a legitimate stage to prepare them for what God had in store.

One would have expected that, when they reached the borders of the Land of Promise about which God had given such a glowing picture, the whole company would stampede in their eagerness to leave the desert and set foot in their new homeland. But no! They proved as reluctant to take possession of their inheritance as many Christians are to take the step of faith and embark on the spiritual experience of which Canaan was the counterpart.

Conflicting reports

At God's command Moses selected twelve leaders, one from each of the tribes, and commissioned them to explore the land of Canaan and bring back a report on the land and its defences (Num 13:1–20). For forty days they thoroughly explored the territory. As a result of their search, there was full agreement among them that it was 'a land flowing with milk and honey', but there the consensus ended. The exploring team was split. A majority report was submitted by what could be called the Timorous Ten—the men of sight and reason. A minority report was presented by the Trustful Two, Joshua and Caleb—the men of faith and vision. And what contrasting pictures they were!

Ten: The land we explored devours those living in it (13:32).

Two: Do not be afraid of the people of the land, because we will swallow them up (14:9).

Ten: The cities are fortified and very large (13:28).

43

Two: Their protection is gone but the Lord is with us (14:9).

Ten: All the people we saw there are of great size.... We seemed like grasshoppers in our own eyes and we looked the same to them (13:32, 33).

Two: We should go up and take possession of the land, for we can certainly do it (13:30).

Ten: We can't (13:31).

Two: We can (13:30).

> Minorities, since time began
>   Have shown the better side of man,
> And often in the lists of time
>   One man has made a cause sublime.

P. L. Dunbar

The explanation of the contrasting viewpoints is not far to seek. Those who submitted the entirely negative and pessimistic majority report looked at the might of their enemies through the magnifying glass of fear and unbelief. The optimistic minority gained a true perspective through their faith in the omnipotent God who had already displayed His power. All twelve had seen exactly the same sights. The Ten viewed God through the difficulties. The Two viewed the difficulties through a God to whom nothing was impossible.

In their report, the majority *impeached God's Word*, treating Him as though He were a man who would lie to them. They *impugned His power*, as though seven small nations would tax His resources. They *doubted His goodness*, as though His plan was working for their destruction. Unbelief is not only short in memory, but defective in eyesight.

44

No sooner had the report been released than panic broke out among the people, 'and the whole assembly talked about stoning them (Joshua and Caleb)' (14:10). 'If only we had died in Egypt, or in this desert,' they wailed. 'Wouldn't it be better for us to go back to Egypt?' (14:3). 'We should choose a leader and go back to Egypt' (14:4).

In the grip of this grasshopper complex, they were so stubborn in their refusal to cross into Canaan that only the appearance of the awesome Shekinah glory restrained them from killing Joshua and Caleb during their last, moving appeal to the nation to put their trust in God.

> Ten men who failed to see God
>   Saw cities impregnably high;
> Two men, looking off unto God
>   Saw doom for those cities draw nigh.
>
> Ten men who failed to see God
>   Discouraged their fellow-men;
> Two men perceived God everywhere!
>   Are you of the two—or the ten?

The negative attitude of the Ten has its modern counterpart. There are always those who discourage others from 'going up to possess the land'. Because they have never experienced it, they assert that no such life of victory is possible. They argue that the Sermon on the Mount, though a beautiful ideal, is not applicable today—its standards are too high for us here and now. It is for people in a coming age. In saying this they forget that God has only one standard for the Christian, and that standard is Christ, the

45

living embodiment and model of the Sermon on the Mount.

These sincere Christians rightly stress the fact that when we were converted we received everything in Christ (Eph 1:3). But their teaching suggests that therefore we have it all in experience. Little provision is made for the necessity of moral endeavour and fighting the good fight of faith. They ignore the fact that those spiritual blessings which are potentially ours in Christ become ours experientially only as we appreciate them by faith.

Because some have gone to unwarranted extremes in their teaching and experience of the Holy Spirit and the possibility of living a Spirit-filled life, there are those who, from the best of motives, discourage others from exploring that important subject, they thus prevent enquirers from discovering all that the Holy Spirit can mean to them—a tragic loss.

I was once asked to preach in an American church on the subject of the ministry of the Spirit. In my message I presented the glorious possibility of a life lived under His control. At the close of the service, an elderly gentleman came down the aisle with extended hand and tears glistening in his eyes: 'And to think that I have been a Christian all these years,' he said, 'and never before did I know all that the Holy Spirit could mean in my life!'

A very solemn responsibility rests on those who, however well-intentioned, 'spread a bad report about the land', simply because they themselves have 'failed to enter in', either through ignorance, fear or prejudice.

The illegitimate desert experience

The legitimate desert experience lost its propriety the moment the Israelites turned back from entering the land at Kadesh-Barnea. From that point on theirs was an attitude of sinful rebellion. They would not take the decisive step, and God ratified their fateful decision by turning them back to life in the desert.

In their unbelief and rebellion they had cried, 'Why is the Lord bringing us to this land only to let us fall by the sword? Our wives and children will be taken as plunder' (Num 14:3). Despite God's gracious purpose for them, what they feared came upon them. God pronounced a solemn sentence:

> In this desert your bodies will fall—every one of you twenty years old or more…who has grumbled against me. Not one of you will enter the land…. As for your children that you said would be taken as plunder, I will bring them in to enjoy the land you have rejected (Num 14:29–31).

Of the Israelites who were over twenty years of age, only Joshua and Caleb, the men of faith, survived to taste the joys and victories of Canaan. The remainder 'fell in the desert', a mute yet eloquent testimony to the seriousness and tragedy of unbelief.

The New Testament parallel is not difficult to discern. Sooner or later the Christian will face his own Kadesh-Barnea crisis, when he has to make a choice. Will he press on to the Canaan life of victory, although it will involve conflict, or will he return to the purposeless and unsatisfying life of the desert? The alternatives are far-reaching in their consequences.

Pursuing the latter course will involve the reluctant Christian in the following frustrations and defects that plagued Israel:

Restlessness: in the desert they had had no settled homes. One day they would be camping beside a refreshing oasis; the next they would be traversing the scorching sands. The Christian who opts for the desert-life will be restless in body and restless in mind. No restful Christians are to be found in the desert.

Discontent: murmuring and complaining against God and His chosen leaders was endemic. When God gave them bread from heaven, they craved flesh and the onions, leeks and garlic of Egypt. Forgetful of their recent cruel slavery, they longed to breathe once more the congenial air of that land. The Christian living in the desert will be preoccupied with his own troubles, and have little heart for fighting God's battles. There are no contented Christians in the desert.

Fruitlessness: it is true that Israel fought and won a few battles while in the desert, but they brought them little advantage, nor did they gain any territory. All the benefit they brought was the right to pass through enemy territory. At the close of forty years of marching and fighting, they were as poor and landless as when they began. The battles fought by the desert Christian are likely to be more battles of rebellion rather than of conquest. There are no fruitful Christians in the desert.

Negativity: the main virtue of the Israelites at this stage was that they were not doing Egyptian things, although they obviously had a secret longing to do them. There was little that was positive and aggressive about their lives. Similarly, many Christians are known mostly by what they don't do. They don't drink or smoke or womanize or dance. But having said that, one has said everything. There is little about them that is distinctive. Their lives are notable for what they abstain from rather than for what they achieve. There are few positive Christians in the desert.

Vacillation: in one sense it was not difficult for God to get Israel out of Egypt, but it was a much greater problem to get Egypt out of Israel. In their journeyings they vacillated between the Red Sea and Jordan, between Egypt and Canaan. One moment they were hankering for the pleasures of Egypt, the next they gazed wistfully into the land flowing with milk and honey.

When in the company of 'worldly' Christians, the desert-dweller would gladly join in their worldly pursuits but for the restraining thought of what others may think or say. Occasionally, when away from home or observation by other Christians, he may make a surreptitious excursion back into Egypt.

On the other hand, in his better moments, at a special convention or crusade, he comes once again to the borders of the Promised Land and longs to enter in, but shrinks back at the cost involved. There are no stable Christians in the desert.

If in this diagnosis the reader recognizes some aspects of his own experience, he can be assured that God has something much better for him. The Spirit of God always desires to lure us from the discouraging life of carnality and self-pleasing, and to lead us into a life of habitual overcoming. *The choice is ours.* We may, if we choose, turn our backs on the old life of failure and longing and lusting, and press on to the satisfied life in Canaan.

The following words which are based on this very incident state the options explicitly:

Today, if you hear his voice, do not harden your hearts as you did in the rebellion, during the time of testing in the desert, where your fathers tested and tried me and for forty years saw what I did. That is why I was angry with that generation, and I said, 'Their hearts are always going astray, and they have not known my ways.' So I declared on oath in my anger, 'They shall not enter into my rest.'

See to it, brothers, that none of you has a sinful, unbelieving heart that turns away from the living God (Heb 3:7–12).

Israel had her last chance and missed it. Never again did that adult generation have an opportunity of crossing into the Promised Land. We, too, should fear to say 'Tomorrow' when God says 'Today'.

Keep me from turning back!
My hand is on the plough, my faltering hand;
But all in front of me is untilled land;
The wilderness and solitary place,
The lonely desert with its interspace.
What harvest have I but this paltry grain,
These dwindling husks, a handful of dry corn;
These poor lean stocks? My courage is outworn.
Keep me from turning back!
The handles of my plough with tears are wet,
The shares with rust are spoiled—and yet, and yet,
    My God, keep me from turning back!

PRINCIPLES OF SUCCESS

Joshua 1:1–11; Ephesians 1:3–10; 1 Corinthians 2:14 – 3:1

The law of God can never bring the soul of man into the Land of Promise, not because there is any defect in it, but because of human infirmity and sin. It is the presence of this evil law in our members which makes obedience to the law of God impossible, filling us with disappointment and unrest, ceaseless striving and perpetual failure.

We must therefore leave the Law as an outward rule of life behind us...that the Divine Joshua may lead us into the Land of Promise.[9]

F. B. Meyer

Captain of Israel's host, and Guide
  Of all who seek the land above,
Beneath Thy shadow we abide,
  The cloud of Thy protecting love;
Our strength, Thy grace; our rule, Thy word,
One end, the glory of the Lord.

By Thine unerring Spirit led,
  We shall not in the desert stray;
We shall not full direction need,
  Nor miss our providential way;
As far from danger as from fear,
While love, almighty love is near.

Charles Wesley

Chapter 5

PRINCIPLES OF SUCCESS

Forty years of aimless wandering lay behind the Israelites. In the providence of God they had come once again to the borders of Canaan. With their camp pitched on the east side of the River Jordan, they were at last ready to cross over into their long-promised inheritance.

But as we have seen, only Joshua and Caleb remained of the adult generation that had turned back at Kadesh-Barnea. All the others had died in the desert, as God had foretold. Even Moses and Aaron who had spent their lives in sacrificial service for their nation were excluded from the land because they failed to honour God before the people—a salutary lesson to those in leadership.

At this critical juncture in the nation's history Joshua was eighty years old, no longer a young man. To him God gave the commission to lead the nation into the Promised Land:

> Moses my servant is dead. Now then, you and all these people get ready to cross the Jordan river into the land I am about to give them—to the Israelites (Josh 1:2).

The rather strange sequence of thought in this verse is not without significance. What is the connection between the two sentences? An important spiritual lesson is symbolized. Moses, whose very name is almost synonymous with the Law (which stands for man's best unaided endeavours), could no more lead Israel into the rest and victory of Canaan, than our best unaided efforts can introduce us to a victorious Christian life. Only our heavenly Joshua can lead us there (Heb 4:8).

It is a matter of common spiritual experience that the full blessing of life in the Christian's Promised Land is not usually realized until, through the disillusioning experiences of the desert-life so poignantly depicted in Romans 7, we are brought to see with despair that we cannot attain holiness through self-effort.

'Moses is dead'! What a daunting prospect those words would conjure up in Joshua's mind. No longer could he lean on his old mentor. He was left with God alone. And who could step into the shoes of a man of such massive stature and personality? He would be engulfed in the sense of his own inadequacy.

When some outstanding leader dies, it always seems as though he or she is irreplaceable. But time soon proves, in a most humbling fashion, that no man is indispensable to the purposes of God. God is dependent on no one human instrument, however great or gifted. God buries His workmen, but His work goes on unhindered by the change in personnel. Moses dies, but God has His Joshua ready to assume leadership.

It is usually God's method to bring a leader into prominence only slowly. As A. W. Tozer remarked,

God rarely projects His chosen servants suddenly into a place of public usefulness. Those who appear to have burst upon the world without previous preparation will be found to have spent a long apprenticeship somewhere, before being entrusted with important work.

Principles of success

Joshua reveals the unchanging principles that underlie success in God's service.

First, there came to Joshua the clear *call of God* (v. 2), a call which always carries with it the assurance of divine enabling. This fact was expressed forcefully by Jethro, father-in-law to Moses, when he was urging him to delegate some of the responsibilities that were wearing him into the ground: 'If you do this and God so commands, you will be able to stand the strain' (Ex 18:23).

The call was reinforced by *the renewed promise of possession* of the land of Canaan (vv. 2, 3). The divine Donor was fully entitled to make the gift, for is He not 'Possessor of heaven and earth?' (Gen 14:19 AV). The legal 'consideration' for the gift is disclosed by the psalmist: 'It was not by their sword that they won the land, nor did their arm bring them victory; it was your right hand, your arm, and the light of your face, *for you loved them*' (Ps 44:3, italics mine). The present-day legal terminology would be, 'In consideration of natural love and affection'. No lawyer would reject such a title.

Thenceforth Israel had an unimpeachable title to the land of Canaan. It was theirs *legally* by gift from God.

The principle of appropriation

Although the land was theirs legally, it became theirs *actually* only when they appropriated it by encircling and walking over it, thus taking possession of it as God had instructed them: 'I will give you every place where you set your foot' (Josh 1:3).

The same principle carries over into the New Testament. Jesus enunciated it when he assured the blind man, 'According to your faith will it be done to you' (Mt 9:29).

In surveying the spiritual blessings available to the Christian in his Promised Land, Paul was so carried away that he burst into a doxology:

> Praise be to the God and Father of our Lord Jesus Christ, who *has blessed us* in the heavenly realms with *every spiritual blessing* in Christ (Eph 1:3, italics mine).

Note that this is not a *promise* to be claimed, but an accomplished *fact* that is to be believed and acted on. Every spiritual blessing has already been given to the weakest believer, not on account of merit, but because he is united to Christ. We enjoy in experience only as many of these as we appropriate, as we believe and make our own.

A young missionary known to the author was having a great struggle at language school to master the difficult Chinese language. One day, in despair, he took his large Chinese Grammar and placing it on the floor, stood on it. Then he prayed, 'Lord you said you would give me every place that the sole of my foot trod on. My feet are on the Chinese Grammar. Give me the Chinese language!'

His symbolical act of faith did not go unrewarded. Through diligent study and application, he gained such proficiency that he became head of that very language school.

> I simply take Him at His word,
> I praise Him that my prayer is heard,
> And take my answer from the Lord,
> I take, He undertakes.

A. B. Simpson

Preparation for possession

The odds against the Israelites were horrendous. Recent archeological studies show that the Hittites, one of the nations of Canaan, were a great and cultured people, sufficiently powerful to rival Assyria or Egypt. It was arrant presumption for this untrained horde of erstwhile slaves to think they could dispossess and exterminate such a confederacy of highly-trained and well-organized nations.

Joshua, therefore, must be encouraged and braced before he was equipped for the conflict ahead. His preparation had both a divine and a human dimension.

On the divine side there was the *assurance of divine endowment and authority:* 'No-one will be able to stand up against you all the days of your life' (Josh 1:5).

God always gives an authority commensurate with the responsibility He delegates. Despite his inward trembling, this assurance of an endowment adequate for the task would fortify and stabilize him.

He was assured of the divine presence. 'As I was with Moses, so I will be with you' (Josh 1:5).

In his appropriation of this promise lay the secret of Joshua's indomitable courage and calm confidence.

There was also *the affirmation of the divine faithfulness:* 'I will never leave you or forsake you' (Josh 1:5) or, as one rendering has it, 'I will not drop you.'

Strengthened by the presence of the God to whom nothing is impossible and who is utterly dependable, the prospect would not look so bleak.

> Faith, mighty faith the promise sees,
>   And looks to God alone,
>   Laughs at impossibilities
>   And cries, 'It shall be done!'

C. Wesley

On the human side, Joshua was four times challenged to *'be strong and courageous'*. Strength and courage are a *sine qua non* in a military leader who is about to engage in battle an enemy who is immeasurably stronger and better equipped. It should be noted that the onus of being strong and courageous is placed on Joshua himself. The Lord knew the unequal battle ahead and so He urged Joshua:

Have I not commanded you? Be strong and courageous. Do not be terrified; do not be discouraged, for the Lord your God will be with you wherever you go (Josh 1:9).

But does it not seem rather a hollow mockery to tell a man in the grip of discouragement, weakness and fear to be strong and courageous and unafraid? Is it not like telling a neurotic person who is consumed with anxiety not to worry?

How could Joshua be strong and courageous in such a hopeless situation? The answer is that all God's commands are enablings. We *can* do all God commands us to do, for He is pledged not to fail or forsake us. Joshua's fearlessness and courage were not self-generated, but sprang from *the realized presence of God*. They were the product of a combination of conscious weakness and constant dependence. In spiritual warfare, courage that does not rest on the consciousness of God's presence and faithfulness is presumption rather than courage. In a somewhat similar situation, Paul assured Timothy, 'God did not give us a spirit of timidity, but a spirit of power, of love and of self-discipline' (2 Tim 1:7).

Many of us, however, like King Uzziah, become *too strong* for God, especially when we are experiencing success in life and service. Of the King it was written: 'He was greatly helped until he became powerful. But after Uzziah became powerful, his pride led to his downfall' (2 Chron 26:15, 16). As a punishment for his pride and sacrilege, the mighty monarch became a loathsome leper.

Joshua was further charged to *practise constant meditation on the Law of God*.

> Be careful to obey all the law my servant Moses gave you; do not turn from it to the right or to the left, that you may be successful wherever you go. Do not let this Book of the Law depart from your mouth; *meditate on it* day and night, so that you may be careful to do everything written in it. *Then you will be prosperous and successful* (Josh 1:7, 8, italics mine).

The written Word of God was to be his manual of

instruction in warfare. Of course he had only the Pentateuch, but consistent consultation and obedience to its provisions would constitute the recipe for prosperity and success. In it he would find his marching orders and plan of campaign. This Book, not his sword, was to be his main equipment for leadership. He must therefore saturate himself in it. If he neglected to do so, his courage would ooze out of his finger-tips when he came to meet his experienced foes.

Meditation is not dreamy reverie, but hard thinking and mature reflection. Paul enjoined this exercise on the Christians in Philippi:

> Whatever is true, whatever is noble, whatever is right, whatever is pure, whatever is lovely, whatever is admirable—if anything is excellent or praiseworthy— think about such things (Phil 4:8).

The tendency in the contemporary world, however, is to immerse ourselves in a different type of literature, or to spend an inordinate amount of time before the television screen, or to have the radio going all day. This often leaves little time for serious reading and genuine meditation on the Word of God. As a result, our spiritual life becomes shallow. Neglect of meditation on Scripture results in an anaemic spiritual life. In point of fact, the life of victory in the Promised Land calls for more Bible study, not less.

It is instructive to compare Ephesians 5:18–20 with Colossians 3:16–17 and to note that the same results in Christian character and human relationships follow from being filled with the Spirit as from being filled with the Word of Christ. The implication is that we will *remain* filled with the Spirit only as long as we constantly meditate on Scripture.

Joshua was urged to *obey the Word of God in every detail.* 'Be careful to obey all the law my servant Moses gave you; do not turn from it to the right or to the left' (Josh 1:7). This injunction is no less important than the previous ones, for disobedience to light given effectively prevents the reception of further light. We are told that the Holy Spirit 'is given to those who obey him'. Disobedience concedes to the devil a vantage point from which he can wage guerilla warfare.

> My Lord, who in the desert fed
> On soul-sustaining heavenly bread,
> Words that were meat and drink to Thee—
> O let them daily nourish me!
>
> And since that sword that served Thee well
> In battling with the powers of hell
> Is even now at hand for me,
> Help me to wield it manfully.

Frank Houghton

Charge to the people

Today is always preparation for tomorrow. The people, as well as their leader, must be prepared for conflict. 'Get your supplies ready,' was the command. 'Three days from now you will cross the Jordan here to go in and take possession of the land the Lord your God is giving you' (v. 11).

Up to this point the daily supply of manna had continued, but in three days' time it would cease. In the desert their food had been provided without any effort on their part, but now they must forage for their own. They would be dependent on obtaining grain from the abandoned storehouses of the people of Jericho.

This affords an interesting lesson. The spiritual food that sufficed for the desert-dwelling Christian is inadequate to support life in the Promised Land with its arduous conflict. For that he will require larger and more frequent meals of 'the old corn of the land'. In Canaan we need to glean from the Word an ever-expanding conception of God Himself, and more intimate familiarity with the details of His plan of campaign.

The 'worldly' or 'carnal' Christian differs from the 'spiritual' believer (1 Cor 3:1) in that the former is largely dependent on human preachers and teachers to provide pre-digested spiritual food. The latter, even if deprived of fellowship with other believers or of helpful preaching, will be able to maintain the spiritual glow because he has learned how to gather sustenance from the Scriptures, directly from God.

A soldier who does not know how to care for his food and his feet will soon be out of active service. We must daily dig into the Scriptures and feed our souls on its great truths—its commands, warnings and reproofs as well as its comforting promises. 'Solid food is for the mature' (Heb 5:14).

THE JORDAN CROSSING

Joshua 2:8–11; 3:1–17; 4:16–18; Romans 6:1–14; 8:13

This crossing of Jordan is the most striking picture you can have of what it means to be crucified with Christ, and buried in His death. We were nailed to that cross in Him, identified with Him (Rom 6:4).... The twofold aspect of our identification with Christ is portrayed by these two lots of stones. As on the one hand twelve stones were buried in the river flood, and on the other, twelve stones were taken from the river bed and carried to the Canaan side as memorials of their separated life to God, so are we taken into the life of our Lord and there buried so far as our relation to sin and this world is concerned; and out of that river-bed of death, we are taken into resurrection and triumphant life.[10]

Jessie Penn-Lewis

The Jordan Crossing

By Jordan's rushing stream I stand;
The rolling tide is deep and wide, I see no way;
I long to reach the Promised Land;
The desert life of inward strife I leave today;
O Lord, from sin grant full release,
Give me Thy perfect peace.

The pillar sheds its glowing light
On corn and wine, on fields that shine in fairest dress;

But turns its cloud of darkest night,
To sighs and tears of weary years, my wilderness.
  With God behind, and God before,
    I'll reach the farther shore.

  I look in vain for Moses' rod,
Yet on the brink I will not shrink nor fear the tide;
  Th' eternal word, the ark of God
Goes on before from shore to shore, the floods divide.
  I reckon I am dead to sin;
    God's word gives peace within.

  I find the corn and wine and oil;
No Egypt's taste, no desert waste, no manna here;
  I reap the richest of the spoil;
My feet now stand upon the land, no foes I fear.
  I trust in what my Joshua saith,
    And fight the fight of faith.

R. Kelso Carter

Chapter 6

THE JORDAN CROSSING

The camp of Israel had removed from Shittim to the banks of the River Jordan. The explorers had returned from their reconnaissance with the reassuring news of the demoralization of the nations of Canaan through hearing of God's interventions on Israel's behalf (2:8–11). Joshua had, in faith, accepted the victory God had promised, and assured the people, 'Tomorrow the Lord will do amazing things among you' (3:5).

The crucial moment had arrived when the nation must choose between the Canaan life or the desert life. So in each generation the Christian is brought to the place where he must choose between the desert life of self-effort, failure and frustration, or life of victory and fulfilment in the Promised Land. There is a Jordan to be crossed in the life of every Christian.

Five phrases that are used of this incident succinctly summarize its teaching:

East of the Jordan—counting the cost (1:15)

Though they were in sight of the Land of Promise, a

rushing torrent separated them from it, for 'the Jordan is in flood all during harvest' (3:15). Before them lay difficulties sufficient to chill the stoutest heart.

First, *Jordan's turbulent waters*, an impassable flood, since there was no bridge and they had no boats. The river is usually about fifty or sixty yards in breadth, but at harvest time, swollen by Hermon's snows, it becomes a turbulent torrent. Could a more unsuitable time have been chosen for a crossing? Humanly it was impossible. They were shut up to God, who gave them a three-day pause, doubtless to allow them time to face the difficulties ahead realistically and count the cost.

Tristram, in his *Land of Israel*, gives this account of a visit to the Jordan which highlights the forbidding prospect Israel faced.

> We were on the banks of the Jordan.... Muddy, swollen and turbid, the stream was far too formidable and rapid for the most adventurous to attempt their intended bathe. Had we arrived a few days sooner, we could not have approached the river at all.... By measurement we found that the river had lately been fourteen feet higher than its present margin, and yet it was still many feet above its ordinary level.[11]

The second and equally daunting problem was *Jericho's threatening walls* which could already be seen in the distance. 'So the people crossed over opposite Jericho' (3:16). This city with its white walls and verdant palm trees held the key to Canaan. So strongly fortified as to be almost impregnable, it guarded all the passes into the interior. The people might well be forgiven if they were as fearful of what lay beyond Jordan as they were of its rushing waters.

It will not be difficult for us at times to envision our own immediate Jordan and threatening Jericho looming up in the distance—a Jericho that might be the fulcrum on which the whole of life turns. It may be a public confession of Christ; an apology that should be tendered; some restitution that should be made; a letter of reconciliation to be written; the termination of some family feud; the correction of some marital disharmony; the relinquishing of some long-cherished resentment; some neglected duty that should be performed. Whatever it is, our personal Jericho must be faced and vanquished if we are to know the rest of Canaan.

Like Israel, we face two alternatives—by a step of faith to cross the Jordan and face Jericho, or to return to the illegitimate and frustrating life of the desert. There is no other course open.

Procedure outlined

Hitherto the nation had been supernaturally guided by the pillar of cloud and fire, but now this was to be withdrawn and they were to know a new experience of guidance. Henceforth they would be guided by the sacred Ark of the Covenant, carried by their own countrymen. In the Promised Land, supernatural manifestation gives place to spiritual heart-exercise and obedience. They had been given no clue as to how the waters would part. It was to be a matter of faith, not sight. God revealed His plan of campaign to Joshua alone, and on the morning of the crossing he outlined the procedure to be followed.

Before they started they were to *sanctify themselves*

66

(3:5). Their preparation was to be spiritual, not military or ceremonial. Their instructions were not to sharpen their swords but to set themselves apart for God's use. Another spiritual principle is illustrated here. God's sovereign intervention on our behalf awaits the discharge of our responsibility. *We fix the time for the display of His power.* 'Consecrate yourselves, for tomorrow the Lord will do amazing things among you' (Josh 3:5). God is not fitful or capricious. When we conform to 'the law of the Spirit' (Rom 8:2), His infinite power is at our service. God's tomorrow of wonders depends on our today of sanctification. It is on man's side that the windows of blessing are bolted. Our consecration withdraws the restricting bolts and the showers are released.

If it be objected that sanctification is God's prerogative, not ours, the answer is that there is also a very real sense in which we must sanctify ourselves. Paul expresses it in these words: 'Since we have these promises, dear friends, let us purify ourselves from everything that contaminates body and spirit, perfecting holiness out of reverence for God' (2 Cor 7:1).

Although God will supply all the power and grace necessary for a holy life there are some things He cannot and will not do for us. The initiative is with us. It involves, negatively, putting away, renouncing all that the Holy Spirit shows is alien to God's holy nature; and positively, the renewal of a complete surrender to Him and His service. When Israel sanctified themselves, they renounced their sin and placed themselves without reservation at God's disposal. They counted on His good faith, and fulfilled their own part. The amazing things soon followed. Their sanctification was the essential human factor in the resulting victory.

The order of the crossing of Jordan was to be as follows: first, the priests with the ark; second, Joshua and the twelve leaders of Israel; third, the people.

At the edge of the Jordan—the step of faith (Josh 3:8)

God is always loyal and faithful to the leaders He appoints, so before embarking on the campaign He honoured His servant Joshua.

> The Lord said to Joshua, 'Today I will begin to exalt you in the eyes of all Israel, so that they may know I am with you as I was with Moses' (Josh 3:7).

Exaltation to high leadership carries its own built-in perils and not everyone survives the test. The way in which Joshua reacted to such an honour was a tribute to his humility and the quality of his life.

When they reached the Red Sea in their trek from Egypt, Israel had found a path already made for them through its waters. No demands were made on their faith. All they had to do was to walk across. Not so at Jordan. Here there was no evidence whatever to their senses that the way would open up before them. They had to 'walk by faith and not by sight'. This is true in Christian experience. As we mature in the Canaan-life, God weans us from sight and shuts us up to faith.

> When we cannot see our way,
> Let us trust and still obey;
> He who bids us forward go
> Cannot fail the way to show.

Tho' the sea be deep and wide,
Tho' a passage be denied,
Fearless let us still proceed,
Since the Lord vouchsafes to lead.

Night with Him is never night,
Where He is, there all is light;
When He calls us, why delay?
They are happy who obey.

T. Kelly

In obedience to Joshua's instructions, the white-robed priests advanced until a thousand yards lay between them and the people. This was partly for the sake of reverence and partly that the ark might be observed by the whole company. Carrying the golden ark with its covering of blue, the priests reached the rushing waters and stood on the very brink of Jordan. It is unlikely that they stood there without trepidation. 'What if nothing happens when we step into the river?' This is always the challenge of unbelief. But at the first touch of their feet, the muddy waters opened and God responded to their step of faith.

The safe crossing of the Jordan is not only a miracle, but a multiple miracle in which a number of factors were involved—the exactness of the timing, the fact that it happened in flood time, that the water was held up for almost a day and that the river-bed was solid enough to allow many thousands to cross.

It may have been that God used a natural phenomenon such as an earthquake to cause a land-slide and dam the river—as happened in 1906 and again in 1927. But whatever the method, it was in keeping with God's sovereign control of nature. The damming of the waters happened by design, not by chance.

Those who believe the Scriptures to be a fully inspired record feel under no necessity to provide an explanation from natural causes for what appears to have been sovereignly ordained by God.

The secret of their successful crossing is contained in the words: 'See, the ark of the covenant of the Lord of all the earth will go into the Jordan ahead of you' (Josh 3:11). The ark of the covenant which housed the two stone tablets on which the Decalogue was inscribed was the visible and tangible sign of God's presence in the nation's midst, and He used it to direct their attention to His invisible leadership. A literal rendering of this verse is: 'Behold the ark of the covenant! The Lord of all the earth is about to proceed before you into Jordan'. Thus it was clear to Israel that Jehovah Himself, and not a golden box, was present to lead them. At every stage the conquest was to be seen as God's victory, a victory of faith.

What the ark was to the Israelite, that and much more, Christ is to us. When the feet of Jesus dipped into the river of death, its waters receded, so that we who are in Him can pass through in safety. When He went down into death, He carried the whole Church in Himself into that death. But it is only as we claim personally our share in the benefits and blessings His death and resurrection gained for us, that the Holy Spirit can make it actual in experience.

At the feet of the Christian who aspires to a closer walk with God and the full Canaan experience, there always flows a Jordan that must be crossed. For Israel it was not a matter of *growing out* of the desert, but of *going over* into Canaan. We do not automatically grow out of the desert experience any more than Israel did. It was the result of a calculating, decisive step of faith.

In the middle of the Jordan—buried with Christ

> The priests who carried the ark of the covenant of the Lord stood firm on dry ground in the middle of the Jordan, while all Israel passed by until the whole nation had completed the crossing on dry ground (Josh 3:17).

This symbolic action is replete with spiritual significance. The descent of the priests into the Jordan finds its counterpart in these verses:

> Don't you know that all of us who were baptised into Christ Jesus were baptised into his death? We were buried with him in baptism into death, in order that, just as Christ was raised from the dead through the glory of the Father, we too may live a new life (Rom 6:3, 4).

It is important to distinguish between the two complementary aspects of the Lord's death—substitution and identification.

The *substitutionary aspect* has in view deliverance from the penalty and guilt of sin. We are delivered from these by believing that on the cross Christ died for us, in our place. How do we know this? Because we feel it? No, because God's Word reveals it, and we rest on what it says. We have no other source of knowledge of the significance of His death.

The *identification aspect* is concerned with deliverance from the tyranny and dominion of sin. We are delivered

71

from these by believing that we were identified with Christ when He died on the cross. What evidence do we have for this? The assurance of the same Word of truth. The same Bible that tells us Christ died *for* us, assures us that we died *with* Christ. If we believe the first statement and have received the promised blessing, we must also, if we are to be consistent, believe the other to be true (Rom 6:6).

This verse teaches that when Christ died, He did not die alone. Just as the whole human race was potentially 'in Adam' when he fell into sin, so the whole body of believers was 'in Christ' when He died on the cross to atone for the sins of the world and to break their power.

All who are the natural descendants of Adam have, without any action on their part, inherited a sinful nature. So all who are the spiritual seed of Christ are heirs to the benefit of all that His death and resurrection secured. It is for us to believe this divinely revealed fact, and to act on it as being true, for it is true.

This is not an attainment of certain advanced Christians, but a fact true of all believers. It was not a crisis which took place at some time in Paul's career through some action or attitude of his. It is true of us whether we believe it or not, and whether we derive any conscious benefit from it or not.

The reason for God identifying 'our old self' with Christ in His death is not far to seek. No house can have two masters. Our former self is incurably wicked and will never abdicate in favour of Christ, so God must deal drastically with the usurper. He passed sentence on him, and that sentence was carried out on Calvary. And now to every Christian seeking deliverance from the power of sin, God says in effect: 'Your old self, the traitor within, the cause of all your trouble, was nailed to Christ's cross. Count on this accomplished fact and act as if it were so.'

But how does this operate in actual experience? Paul exhorts us: 'In the same way, count yourselves dead to sin but alive to God in Christ Jesus' (Rom 6:11). In doing this we can count on the aid of the Holy Spirit. 'If *by the Spirit* you put to death the misdeeds of the body, you will live' (Rom 8:13, italics mine).

We cross Jordan in experience when we concur in God's sentence on our unregenerate selves and consent to die; when we hand him over to the Holy Spirit to execute the sentence of death in us.

To 'reckon' or 'count' (Rom 6:11) is not to imagine something to be true which is really not true, but to count on something which is really true. It is not like a legal fiction, nor does it have anything to do with our feelings. It is a mathematical word meaning 'to compute or calculate'. It is the attitude of mind in which we count a thing to be true for reasons as sure as that two and two make four. Spiritually, it means to count as true what the Bible says is true, whatever our feelings.

But a dead man is not of much service to God or man. Counting oneself dead to sin is a purely negative though necessary aspect of truth. This was illustrated at Jordan by the fact that the priests did not remain in the midst of the river.

Up out of Jordan—risen with Christ

> Command the priests carrying the ark of the Testimony
> to come up out of the Jordan…. And the priests came up
> out of the river (Josh 4:16, 18).

This too has its New Testament parallel, for 'If we
have been united with him in his death, we will
certainly also be united with him in his resurrection'
(Rom 6:5).

> Buried with Christ and raised with Him
> too,
> What is there left for me to do?
> Simply to cease from struggling and strife,
> Simply to walk in newness of life.
> Glory be to God.
>
> Risen with Christ, my glorious Head,
> Holiness now the pathway I tread,
> I am from bondage utterly freed,
> Reckoning self as dead indeed.
> Glory be to God.
>
> *T. Ryder*

How do we know that we were united with Him in
His resurrection? Once again, we simply accept in
faith the sure Word of God, and count on it being true
in our particular case. From Calvary there flows a dual
stream—a stream of death, breaking the power of sin
over us, and a stream of life, enabling us to live a new
life.

The crossing of the Jordan involved a definite and
decisive action of the collective will of the nation. So it

is with the individual believer. When Jesus confronted the man with the withered hand and commanded him to stretch it out, the man might well have demurred saying that he did not feel the power to stretch it out. But instead, he counted on the Lord's good faith, and willed to stretch it out. Between the act of willing and the act of stretching out his hand, came the Lord's enabling power in response to his faith. So will it be with us.

A helpful illustration of this important though not easily grasped truth, is Abraham Lincoln's Act of Emancipation which freed America's slaves.

The moment Lincoln signed his name to that historic document, every slave in the United States of America was legally free. No master had the right or power any longer to keep him in bondage. But every slave though legally free was not immediately liberated experientially. Before this took place, several things must happen.

* The slave must hear the liberating news. The important thing was knowing, not feeling.
* Next he must believe the good news.
* He must then count on the news being true, not only of slaves in general, but with respect to his own case in particular.
* Then he must assert his liberty and refuse any longer to be a slave of his former master.
* In doing this, he could count on all the power of the legislature of the United States of America being behind him as he refused further bond service.

So with the believer. In His own blood Christ signed our Act of Emancipation. Our part on hearing this good news is to believe it, count on its being true in our case, and refuse to be any longer under the heel of Satan and sin. In thus claiming our freedom, and saying 'No' to sin, we can count on all the power of the risen Christ being behind us.

No longer need we be powerless in our service for God. Through our union with Christ in His resurrection, we are now 'alive unto God', that is, responsive to Him—alive to prayer, testimony, calls for service.

Clean over Jordan—newness of life

> The priests...stood firm on dry ground in the middle of the Jordan, while all Israel passed by until the whole nation had completed the crossing on dry ground (Josh 3:17).

No sooner had the priests come up out of the river than the waters rolled back, as cold and forbidding as ever—but not one of the nation was missing, all had made the crossing.

There was a *definiteness* about the whole operation. Jordan was now the clear and definite boundary between the desert and Canaan. They had no need to ask, 'Are we over the Jordan?' Nor will we need to ask a similar question when we have taken that definite step of faith.

There was a *finality* about it. Between them and their old life of bondage in Egypt and failure and frustration in the desert, lay Jordan's swirling flood. They were shut in with their enemies with no possibility of retreat. Those who have entered on the Canaan-life can look back to see the river of Christ's death flowing between them and the old life of sin.

There was *newness* about it. For the nation, a totally new life had begun. There was better food. Manna gave place to fruit, milk, honey, corn.

There was a better rest. No longer were they wandering aimlessly in the barren desert, but lived in their own comfortable homes.

They had a better song on their lips and in their hearts.

They experienced more consistent victory in their warfare.

THE UNSEEN COMMANDER

Joshua 4:4–8; 5:2–10; 13–15; Colossians 2:11–13

Joshua was alone, prayerfully contemplating what the next step should be, when suddenly there appeared before him 'a man with a drawn sword'. Joshua challenged him....

This was an event of profound importance, and the following four points should be carefully considered: that the man who appeared was a warrior; that Joshua was prepared to fight; that Joshua knew of only two sides, 'for' and 'against'; and that the man warrior announced that he was more than man; that He was none other than the Captain of all God's angelic hosts; and that for the conflict now about to begin, He had come not merely to direct the army of Israel, but to fight for and with it.

Now every part of this incident is relevant to the church of God and to the individual Christian. God in Christ appears in many aspects to His people, and always in the manner most suited to the circumstances and need of the hour.[12]

W. Graham Scroggie

Hark, how the watchmen cry!
Attend the trumpet's sound!
Stand to your arms, the foe is nigh,
The powers of hell surround:

78

Who bow to God's command,
  Your arms and hearts prepare!
The day of battle is at hand!
  Go forth to glorious war.

Go up with Christ your Head,
  Your Captain's footsteps see;
Follow your Captain and be led
  To certain victory.
  All power to Him is given,
  He ever reigns the same;
Salvation, happiness and heaven
  Are all in Jesus' name.

Jesus' tremendous name
  Puts all our foes to flight:
Jesus, the meek and angry Lamb
  A Lion is in fight.
  By all hell's host withstood,
  We all hell's hosts o'erthrow;
And conquering them, through Jesu's blood,
  We still to conquer go.

Charles Wesley

Chapter 7

THE UNSEEN COMMANDER

The key to victory in the whole Canaan campaign lay in the conquest of the fortress city of Jericho, whose white walls were clearly visible in the distance. As long as Jericho's walls remained unbreached, the whole land was safe from invasion.

On the banks of the Jordan Joshua and his people had faced an impossible situation—transporting a nation across a swiftly-flowing, flooded river without either boats or bridges. Now they confronted another obstacle no less formidable—impregnable Jericho. It seemed just as impossible a hurdle as the Jordan crossing.

But they had safely crossed their Rubicon (a small river that Julius Caesar crossed in 49 BC, which committed him to a great civil war). Israel were confined in enemy territory, irrevocably committed to a war to the death. The flooded Jordan effectively cut off all possibility of retreat. They had no homes or fortresses into which they could repair. All the older and more experienced warriors were dead. It would be difficult to imagine a less promising situation.

80

Palm-girt Jericho with its strong walls, was so strongly fortified that it was virtually impregnable. J. B. Graybill writes:

> Jericho is probably the oldest city in the world. Its strategic site by a ford of the Jordan controlled the ancient trade routes to the East. After crossing the river these branched out, one going towards Bethel and Shechem in the north, another, westward to Jerusalem, and a third to Hebron in the south. Thus Jericho controlled the access to the hill country of Palestine from Transjordan.... The city's location made its capture the key to the invasion of the central hill country.[13]

There is no certainty about the exact position of the Jericho of Joshua's day, but there is fairly common agreement that it was not a large city—more a large fortress than a city in our sense of the word. Some scholars think it covered no more than ten acres. It was, however, a formidable fortress and equipped to withstand a long siege.

Joshua had received no special instructions from God concerning the mode of attack he should adopt. Moses was dead and there was no one with whom he could helpfully consult, so he decided to reconnoitre by himself to discover the strenghts and weaknesses of the fortress. He well knew that the very existence of the nation was at stake, for defeat would mean extermination. The burden of leadership lay heavily upon him and he must find some solution to the problem.

The obvious method of attacking a walled city would be by the use of battering rams and scaling ladders, but they had no such instruments of war.

Some alternative strategy must be adopted. So Joshua made his way, doubtless by night, to Jericho, little dreaming that he was about to face the determining crisis of his life. Such crises do not announce themselves beforehand!

But before Joshua and Israel were in a position to capture Jericho, three significant things must take place.

Circumcision

First, *circumcision, the sign of God's covenant with Israel, must be revived* (Gen 17:9–14; Josh 5:2–8).

During the forty years in the desert the rite had been neglected, and thus the covenant had been broken. The abrogated covenant must be reinstituted with the unanimous consent of all the people. No males under thirty-eight years old were circumcised and, in New Testament language, Israel was out of fellowship with God, and thus had forfeited His protection, although He extended His mercy.

At Gilgal, the place of their first encampment on entering Canaan, this mark of separation was renewed and all males were circumcised (5:2–8). 'Today I have rolled away the reproach of Israel from you', was the Lord's cryptic statement. (The name Gilgal means, 'rolling'.) This may have referred to the removal of the stigma of being slaves, or perhaps to the taunts of the Egyptians that had followed them. But more probably it refers to their breach of the covenant and desire for the idolatrous worship of Egypt. But now they were a nation of freemen, once more in covenant relationship with God. They were re-identified as the people of

God, having renewed their commitment to God's covenant with Abraham.

It must not be overlooked that their obedience in this matter involved *a test of faith*. Imagine a military commander incapacitating his whole army. For several days the greater part of the male population was immobilized, and the nation was at the mercy of the fierce and heavily armed men of Jericho. From a military point of view, Joshua's obedience to the Lord's command put the whole operation in jeopardy. Israel was a 'sitting duck', for the men would be in pain and helpless for several days until their wounds healed. But the faith of the nation had been strengthened by the divine intervention at the crossing of Jordan, and they trusted God to protect them in this hour of need.

This rite of circumcision holds spiritual significance for the Christian who desires to experience victory in his life. 'Circumcise yourselves to the Lord' were the Lord's words through Jeremiah to the men of Judah and Jerusalem. 'Circumcise your hearts' (Jer 4:4). Such heart circumcision marks our separation to the Lord (Rom 12:1).

The Passover

Next, *the Passover Festival must be observed* (5:10). This could be celebrated only by a people in covenant relationship with God, so during the desert years it had not been observed. So, as Francis Schaeffer remarked, the two sacraments were brought together at this moment of history.

The annual ceremony of the Passover was designed to recall to the minds of successive generations that they had been redeemed by blood. A whole generation had lost their grip on this important fact, and now that the covenant had been renewed at Gilgal, the rite could once again be observed. This was only the third occasion on which the Passover had been kept. The second had been held on the first anniversary of the institution (Num 9:4, 5).

In these two rites we may discern a parallel with Christian baptism and the Lord's Supper—one individual, and the other corporate; one an initiatory rite, the other a regularly repeated sacrament. The New Testament makes reference to baptism as the Christian's circumcision: 'In him you were also circumcised, in the putting off of the sinful nature, not with a circumcision done by the hands of men but with the circumcision done by Christ, having been buried with him in baptism and raised with him through your faith in the power of God, who raised him from the dead' (Col 2:11–13).

The lesson for us is that God intends that Calvary shall never be very far away from our thoughts. The cross must be central, for not only is it the ground of our salvation but it is the weapon of our victory over the powers of darkness. 'They overcame him (Satan) by the blood of the Lamb' (Rev 12:11). Paul expressed his commitment to this priority when he claimed, 'I resolved to know nothing while I was with you except Jesus Christ and him crucified' (1 Cor 2:2).

On the day following the Passover everyone ate the food of the land, taken doubtless from the granaries abandoned by the people who had crowded into Jericho. After two more days, the manna which had been their mainstay for forty years, disappeared as suddenly as it had begun—a significant miracle of timing.

Both manna and corn are recognized in the New Testament as types of the Lord Jesus who is the living bread sent down from heaven (Jn 6:51). One writer has said, 'The change from manna to grain speaks of the corresponding change that comes to the Christian in his Promised Land in his apprehension of the person and work of the Saviour.' He may have known Him as Saviour, now he knows and recognizes Him as Lord and Master.

The new Commander

The third significant event leading up to the conquest of Jericho was the conquest of Joshua himself. While he was walking around the walls of the city, thinking his own thoughts and making his own plans, he had no idea that just where he stood he would have a personal encounter with God.

Suddenly, a mysterious visitor with a drawn sword in his hand confronted him. Like a good military man, Joshua's hand flew to his own sword, and he threw out the challenge:

> 'Are you for us or for our enemies?'
> 'Neither', was the reply, 'but as commander of the army of the Lord I have now come' (Josh 5:13–15).

Neither ally nor enemy, but Commander.

> Then Joshua fell face down to the ground in reverence, and asked him, 'What message does my Lord have for his servant?'

'Take off your sandals, for the place where you are standing is holy.'

The revelation of God always brings us to our knees in contrition and reverence, and the vision usually comes when we look away from our petty preoccupations to the Lord of glory.

Even prostration was not all that was required of Joshua. In the East, when approaching a person of eminent sanctity, it was a mark of reverence to remove one's sandals. So Joshua was commanded to take off his sandals. Only when he had completely surrendered to the Commander and handed back his command was God able to unfold His plan of campaign. Henceforth Joshua was to fight with a sword that was 'bathed in heaven' (Is 34:5).

There are points of similarity between this experience of Joshua, and that of Moses at the burning bush (Ex 3:5). At the beginning of their respective leadership responsibilities, God appeared personally to each of them. Each removed his sandals as a mark of deep reverence for the holiness of God, for each had the spiritual wisdom to recognize that he was in the presence of God.

'When we come into the presence of God, we may not carry on our feet the dirt that clings to us through our contact with the world, but must lay aside all uncleanness and earthliness'.[14]

'Let us draw near to God with a sincere heart... having our hearts sprinkled to cleanse us from a guilty conscience, and having our bodies washed with pure water' (Heb 10:22).

Joshua had the discernment to realize that the

heavenly Visitor had not come merely to supplement his military activities, but to entirely *supplant* him as leader. Not to help, but to control. Israel was now under a new, though unseen, Supreme Commander.

We must never think of our Lord merely as an Ally on whom we can call for help, although He is that. He must be recognized and consulted as Commander and He will accept no other role. Our human strength and wisdom are no match for our wily adversary, but the cross spelt his defeat. Christ can perform His mighty works only when we concede Him His rightful place, as Joshua did when he said, 'What message does *my Lord* have for his servant?' (5:13, italics mine).

When one has been in a top leadership position, it is not easy to be displaced in favour of another. But Joshua's concern was with the welfare of the nation and the capture of Jericho—not with his own prestige. Had he refused to submit to the new Leader, he would still face the impossible situation. It would not go away, but he would have to meet it with only his own resources. He might study military strategy and take lessons in scaling walls, but he did not have the resources to gain the victory, and he knew it. So he willingly accepted the transfer of authority and rendered loyal obedience to the Commander who dictated both strategy and tactics. His responsibility was to keep sensitively in touch with Him and to execute His orders.

It is of interest that to those who accept God's sovereignty, the Lord becomes just what they need at that particular time. To Abraham the pilgrim God revealed Himself as a traveller; to the resistant Jacob, as a wrestler; to the soldier Joshua, as a warrior with sword drawn; to the afflicted, God reveals Himself as the God of all comfort. He is always the complement of our present need.

The invisible Commander was now responsible for the protection of the defenceless nation. The burden was lifted from Joshua's shoulders. But it was one thing for him to surrender leadership in principle, and quite another to implement it in practice. The test was not long in coming—it never is.

The unorthodox strategy dictated by the Commander was contrary to both commonsense and military experience. Whoever heard of marching and shouting bringing down impregnable city walls? Hudson Taylor wrote:

> Our Lord's commands sometimes appeared strange, and those to whom they were addressed could not always see the reasons which led to them, or the results consequent on obedience. At times it might have been urged that they were impracticable, as for instance, when He told the man with the withered arm to stretch it forth. Faith, however, 'laughs at impossibilities', and obedience raises no questions.[15]

Then, as now, every fresh step of faith we take leaves one open to a fresh test. But in this case Joshua had a divine promise of victory on which to plant his feet. He returned from his reconnaissance no longer a burdened man. Anxiety had vanished and the assurance of victory was in his heart.

There are several lessons of contemporary value that we may glean from this incident.

Before Joshua could stand dauntless before the foe, he must stand devoutly before his God. His eyes must be directed away from the seemingly impossible task to the God with whom nothing is impossible. It is easy to be so preoccupied with the opposing forces that God is obscured.

Joshua had to surrender his command and pass the reins of authority to Another; to renounce his own strategy and tactics except as they coincided with those of the Commander. On this personal crisis the whole campaign depended. The most significant moments in life are those in which God is pleased to reveal Himself. God's self-revelation is progressive and He is always revealing Himself in fresh ways. Each new revelation meets a new need. Each new act of obedience opens the way to further blessing.

With the transfer of his command, Joshua transferred his responsibility for the success of the campaign. Up to this point, everything had depended on his own wisdom and skill. After the crisis, he was no longer anxious, and spread an atmosphere of faith and soundly-based optimism.

In public Joshua was leader, and God supported him in his leadership—but in private he was the servant, obediently seeking the Commander's plan of campaign and carrying it out with meticulous care.

Wherever there is a forbidding Jericho, there is an experienced and undefeated Commander. We need never fight our battles alone. He has at His disposal a third force, a heavenly army which He directs. Instead of being preoccupied with the impregnability of our Jerichos, let us rest in the omnipotence of God.

THE CONQUEST OF JERICHO

Joshua 6:1–20; Psalm 44; Ephesians 6:10–18; Hebrews 11:30

There is a final lesson in the conquest of Jericho. The real battle about which we are reading is not with the Canaanites at all. It is with God's own people.... All this blowing of trumpets, all of this numerical listings of sevens, were not really necessary to knock down a little wall. God was not frantically collecting His energy so that He could destroy Jericho. He could have just spoken and Jericho would have vaporized. The real battle of Jericho was with the human heart, not with the wall of a city. God was seeking to overcome the Israelites rather than simply to overcome the Canaanites.[16]

Paul E. Toms

Without a Blow

I'm more than conqueror thro' His Blood,
    Jesus saves me now;
I rest beneath the shield of God,
    Jesus saves me now.
I go a kingdom to obtain,
I shall through Him the victory gain
    Jesus saves me now.

Before the battle-lines are spread,
    Jesus saves me now,

Before the boasting foe is dead,
   Jesus saves me now.
I win the fight though not begun,
I'll trust and shout, still marching on,
   Jesus saves me now.

I'll ask no more that I may see,
   Jesus saves me now,
His promise is enough for me,
   Jesus saves me now.
Though foes be strong and walls be high,
I'll shout, He gives the victory,
   Jesus saves me now.

Why should I ask a sign from God?
   Jesus saves me now,
Can I not trust the precious blood?
   Jesus saves me now.
Strong in His word, I meet the foe
And, shouting, win without a blow,
   Jesus saves me now.

Joseph Parker

Chapter 8

THE CONQUEST OF JERICHO

Joshua, without any doubt, in consultation with his Commander-in-Chief, had drawn up an overall plan of campaign. He would aim to drive a wedge into the centre of the land, west from Jerusalem, thus employing the ancient military strategy. 'Divide and conquer'. He then planned to wheel south to liquidate the southern foe, and then later mop up what remained of the northern armies. It is a striking tribute to his God-guided military genius, that by adopting exactly the same strategy, General Allenby was successful in occupying Palestine in World War I.

But first there was Jericho. God had planned the capture of the fortress with a triple purpose in mind. First, it would test the rebellious nation's obedience to God. Second, it would deepen the fear already clutching at the heart of the people of the land. Third, when victory came, altogether apart from military prowess, it would convince God's people that the overthrow of Jericho was entirely a victory of faith. They might have been excused for questioning the validity of so quixotic a strategy as that suggested by the

Commander, but their obedience was complete. It is to their credit that their faith survived the test of what seemed an irrational plan.

Important lessons for our spiritual warfare with Satan and the powers of darkness, can be learned from this venture and victory of faith.

Theirs was a faith that rested in God

The whole operation was a venture of faith that involved taking a tremendous risk. In the face of unequal odds they were relying on God's proved faithfulness. In the suggested strategy, there was no obvious connection between the means and the end. No weapons were to be employed, no sappers to undermine the walls, and no assault to be launched. 'By faith the walls of Jericho fell' (Heb 11:30).

Victory came through divine intervention alone

After they had burned their bridges behind them and staked all on the faithfulness of God, He gave them a repeated promise of victory: 'Then the Lord said to Joshua, "See, *I have delivered* Jericho into your hands, along with its king and its fighting men"' (Josh 6:2, italics mine). Note the tense of the italicized words, 'I have delivered'. On God's part the victory was already as good as an accomplished fact.

It should be observed that the encircling of the fortress was a *religious* rather than a merely military exercise. The victory was won, not because the Hebrews were braver, or more numerous, or better equipped, or had better organization than the army of

Jericho. It was wholly of God and resulted from loyal obedience to His orders. Under Joshua's inspiring leadership, the new-found faith of the nation came into operation, and they were rewarded accordingly.

> So let it be. In God's own might
> We gird us for the coming fight,
> And strong in Him whose cause is ours,
> In conflict with unholy powers,
> We grasp the weapons He has given—
> The Light and Truth and Love of heaven.

J. G. Whittier

It was a faith that obeyed implicitly

The order of the unseen Commander was that they encircle the city once a day for six days, and seven times on the seventh day (Josh 6:3, 4), a command that imposed considerable strain on their obedience and loyalty to God.

As the people had not themselves heard the divine order of the day, or seen the new Commander, it was Joshua, the visible leader, who must take the initiative and infuse his own faith and optimism into the nation. The communication of faith to his subordinates is one of the prime responsibilities of a spiritual leader.

Unbelief and disobedience have always shackled omnipotence. Of Jesus it is recorded that in His home town 'he did not do many miracles there because of their lack of faith' (Mt 13:58). Faith is not credulity, for it is grounded on the infallible word of God. Nothing is impossible to the one who relies on 'the God who calls into existence the things that do not exist'.

94

No matter how inscrutable and imprudent the Lord's commands might seem, it was for Joshua to be a model of unquestioning obedience; to rest on the promises given, although the means seemed inadequate for the end. He was left little scope for originality or genius, but had endless opportunity for the exercise of faith and obedience. The fact that the people followed his lead in this bizarre exercise was evidence of the charisma God had imparted to him (6:13–15).

The non-military character of the siege and march was demonstrated by the fact that discordant rams' horns were to be blown—not silver trumpets. The reason for this was that the latter instruments were used to summon the nation to war, while the rams' horns called them to worship. It was to be God's victory, not man's.

It is noteworthy that in both Scripture and in Christian experience God rarely justifies or interprets His commands in advance. To do so would be to rob faith of its opportunity. Jesus stated an axiom of the faith-life when He said, 'You do not realize now what I am doing, but later you will understand' (Jn 13:7).

It was a faith that was disciplined

Joshua had commanded the people, 'Do not give a war-cry, do not raise your voices, do not say a word until the day I tell you to shout. Then shout!'...They did this for six days (Josh 6:10, 14).

A march of this nature would doubtless bring ridicule from the troops on the walls of the city and ridicule is hard to endure when one doubts the wisdom of the course being followed.

95

What would be the most stringent test for a nation notorious for its murmuring and complaining? Would it not be the discipline of silence? No taunts, no jeers, no words of defiance—no criticism of strategy or tactics—complete silence. It requires little imagination to picture the confusion that would reign if everyone were free to air his views on the strategy being adopted for the overthrow of this fortress! Unbridled criticism and airing of doubts would soon paralyse the nerve of faith. They would have talked themselves out of faith on the first day, for unbelief is unbelievably contagious. There was great spiritual and psychological wisdom in the muzzling of any expressions of unbelief, for this would have afforded a bridgehead for the adversary of which he would have made good use.

As for the inhabitants of Jericho, after the first two or three days, the silent, marching army must have produced a strange effect on a people whose morale had already been undermined. The virile young men of Israel could afford to be silent, for they were inwardly relying on the promise of their omnipotent God who had so convincingly demonstrated His power.

There is a place for silence in the Christian life, difficult though it is to secure it in our electronic age. 'The Lord is in his holy temple; let all the earth be silent before him' (Hab 2:20).

It was a faith that persevered

'They did this for six days. On the seventh day, they got up at daybreak and marched around the city seven times in the same manner' (Josh 6:14). And as they neared the end of the thirteenth circuit, the walls of the city were as stout and forbidding as ever! There was not the slightest visual evidence that their collapse was imminent.

This must have been a tremendous test to the young men itching to pit their strength against that of the Canaanites. To do nothing but wait for God's time is much more difficult than taking matters into our own hands.

This incident has much to teach us in the realm of long-unanswered prayer. Many prayers are not answered because we have not yet completed the thirteenth circuit of our personal Jericho. Ophelia Browning has interpreted this truth very beautifully in her poem which has comforted many:

> Unanswered yet, the prayer your lips have pleaded
> In agony of heart these many years?
> Does faith begin to fail? Is hope departing?
> And think you all in vain those falling tears?
> Say not the Father has not heard your prayer,
> You shall have your desire, sometime, somewhere.
>
> Unanswered yet, though when you first presented
> This one petition at the Father's throne,
> It seemed you could not wait the time of asking,
> So urgent was your heart to make it known?
> Though years have passed since then, do not despair,
> The Lord will answer you, sometime, somewhere.
>
> Unanswered yet? Nay, do not say ungranted,
> Perhaps your part is not yet fully done!
> The work began when first your prayer was uttered,
> And God will finish what He has begun.
> If you will keep the incense burning there,
> His glory you shall see, sometime, somewhere.

Unanswered yet? Faith cannot be unanswered,
Her feet are firmly planted on the Rock.
Amid the wildest storms she stands undaunted,
Nor quails before the loudest thunder-shock.
    She knows Omnipotence has heard her prayer,
    And cries, 'It shall be done!' sometime, somewhere.

It was a faith expressed in a shout of victory

Even after they had completed the thirteenth circuit, the walls remained intact until they voiced the shout of faith.

> When the priests sounded the trumpet blast, Joshua commanded the people, 'Shout! For the Lord has given you the city!'...When the trumpets sounded, the people shouted, and at the sound of the trumpet, when the people gave a loud shout, the wall collapsed; so that every man charged straight in, and they took the city (Josh 6:16, 20).

The fortifications crumbled before their very eyes and Jericho lay naked and helpless before the judgement of God.

It is of the nature of faith that it believes and rejoices in advance of realization. Every step around Jericho had been a step of appropriation by faith. But the climax came with the mighty shout, the release of long pent-up emotion, which was the outward expression of their inward confidence in God. It must be noted that the shout of faith arose *before* the walls showed any sign of collapse, not after. It would be easy to shout afterwards. Once again, in the second impossible situation, they had risked everything on the faithfulness of God and their faith received its reward.

A magnificent example of the shout of faith is told of Robert Moffatt, father-in-law of David Livingstone. For seven years Moffat had been engaged in missionary work in Bechuanaland, but with no visible results.

In those days mails to and from Scotland, his homeland, took six months. In the middle of the year his home church wrote inquiring what they could send him as a Christmas present. As yet there was not a single convert, but in sublime faith Moffatt replied, 'A communion service.' When it arrived at Christmas, was it put to use? Of course it was! That letter had been his shout of faith after he had encircled his Jericho for seven years. God could not disappoint His trusting servant and many new believers joined the missionary in using that communion service to celebrate the Lord's death.

The exact cause of the collapse of the walls is not stated but one thing is clear. It was a miracle as well as a parable, as are most of God's miracles. 'It was not by their sword that they won the land,' said the psalmist, 'nor did their arm bring them victory; it was your right hand, your arm, and the light of your face, for you loved them' (Ps 44:3).

That fact implied another, namely, that God in handing over Jericho to Israel, was executing judgement against the city. The Hebrew name of the city means 'yellow', and is supposed to identify it with the worship of the moon and the moon goddess. This was the same as the Phoenician goddess Ashtoreth or Astarte, the Aphrodite of the Greeks, and the Venus of the Romans. 'In every land the worship of this goddess was a synonym for licentiousness.'[17]

Various theories of the collapse of the wall have

been advanced—the pressure of the crowds upon it; the effect of the army marching around it in step; the vibration of the sound waves, as when a certain note sung by an opera star shatters a glass. An earthquake at Jericho in 1930 produced similar effects. In these cases, the miracle lay in God's supernatural use of the natural.

But whatever explanation of the phenomenon is advanced, there is no alternative, if the record is to be accepted, to the belief that it was a mighty miracle of the intervention of God on behalf of His obedient people.

Two things must be accounted for: first, the fact that the walls collapsed in the very way and at the exact moment that God had foretold (Josh 6:5). Whatever else it was, it was a miracle of timing.

Second, an explanation must be found for the fact that all the wall of the city collapsed *except the section occupied by the house of Rahab the prostitute* (Josh 6:20–25). If the cause were an earthquake, then it acted with strange discrimination in sparing Rahab and her family and home!

It was a faith that gave God the glory

The Lord had clearly stipulated that none of the booty from the sack of Jericho was to be taken by the victorious army. 'Keep away from the devoted things, so that you will not bring about your own destruction by taking any one of them.... All the silver and gold and the articles of bronze and iron are sacred to the Lord' (Josh 6:18, 19).

So in obedience, 'they put the silver and gold and

the articles of bronze and iron into the treasury of the Lord's house' (Josh 6:24). They were not to profit from the triumph, as though they had won it. They were not to be enriched by anything that came out of the accursed city. They could claim no credit for 'by faith the walls of Jericho fell' (Heb 11:30).

The miracle achieved two ends: it inspired Israel with renewed confidence in God as they embarked on what was obviously going to be a long and arduous campaign. It also struck further terror into the hearts of an already demoralized enemy and psychologically conditioned them for defeat.

The dire judgement visited on Jericho served as a visual demonstration to both Israel and the Canaanite nations of God's abhorrence of polytheism and all the moral pollution that accompanied it. J. J. Davies writes:

Israel on several occasions was warned that if she became like the Canaanites, she too would be punished. Therefore, rather than this command and its fulfilment being in conflict with the New Testament, it is after all, a complement to the theological and moral principles of Scripture as a whole. God is a holy God. He demands that sin be punished. The Lord reserves the right to punish sin wherever it is found, whether it be in the immediate destruction of a city or the condemnation of a sinner at final judgment. It is only by the mercy and grace of God that any sinner is permitted to live his life completely.[18]

With the light shed by the circumstances surrounding this resounding victory, it remains for us to face our personal Jerichos and to shout the shout of faith over them. Once we cross our Jordan and enter our own Promised Land, we are confronted at once with the devil and his deeply entrenched hosts. The only way of victory over him is the way of faith.

What is our personal Jericho? Unconfessed sin? Unanswered prayer for members of family or friends? Some stubborn church or mission problem? Some seemingly insoluble marital tangle? Some wrong relationship or unsubdued sin? Some psychological weakness? The Jericho of fear? Some act of restitution?

Is it fear of exposure? During an evangelistic crusade in the author's home city, he was approached by a young man under deep conviction of sin. He confessed that he had given false evidence in a court case which had resulted in considerable damages being wrongly awarded. He asked what he should do about it.

I told him that if he wished to get right with God, he would have to confess his sin and be prepared to make restitution. He was very fearful and hesitant, but when I offered to accompany him he agreed to go to the Insurance Office that had been defrauded.

The manager informed us that the case had been referred back to the Head Office in another city, so he would have to consult them. The young man offered to make restitution as he was able.

In a few days we received a summons to the Insurance Office. The manager said he had received advice from his head office and then proceeded to give the young man a tongue-lashing he would not soon forget. He made no demand for restitution but as we rose to leave the office he gave the young man a strong kick and said, 'Never do such a thing again, or you will not get off so easily.'

He learned his lesson and became a good Christian and respected citizen.

Are you facing an impossible situation?

> 'Twas most impossible of all
> That here in me sin's reign should cease;
> Yet shall it be, I know it shall;
> Jesus I trust Thy faithfulness,
> If nothing is too hard for Thee,
> All things are possible to me.
>
> All things are possible to God;
> To Christ the power of God in man;
> To me when I am all renewed,
> In Christ am fully formed again,
> And from the reign of sin set free,
> All things are possible to me.
>
> All things are possible to God;
> To Christ, the power of God in me;
> Now shed Thy mighty self abroad,
> Let me no longer live but Thee;
> Give me this hour in Thee to prove
> The sweet omnipotence of love.

C. Wesley

Today, as you stand facing your daunting Jericho, turn your eyes away from it to your Commander who knows your problem and has promised victory. Say with Paul when he was facing one of his Jerichos: 'Keep up your courage, men, for I have faith in God that it will happen just as he told me' (Acts 27:25).

Is God calling us to a new step of faith? Do we need to renew our surrender to our Commander-in-Chief?

Have we exhausted the possibilities of what God can do in and through us? Let us not be content to live on the lower levels of mediocrity.

Let us recapture William Carey's vision. It is recorded that his earliest vision was to translate the Bible into the Bengali language. Then God seemed to be saying, 'Translate the Bible into the Bengali language.' Then God seemed to be saying, 'Translate the Bible into the chief languages of India.'

His famous Nottingham sermon that sparked the modern missionary movement comes vividly to mind:

> Thou shalt see greater things than these.
> Enlarge the place of thy tent!
> Stretch forth the curtains of thy habitations!
> Lengthen thy cords! Strengthen thy stakes!
> Expect great things from God,
> Attempt great things for God!
> Dare a bolder programme!
> Dwell in an ampler world!
> Launch out into the deep!

The Voice rang through Carey. The vision was blinding. Have you seen the vision, heard the voice? Will you pay the price?

PERILS OF THE PROMISED LAND

Joshua 7:1–26; 8:1–23; 9:1–21; 10:1–15; Acts 5:1–10

The sequence of events at the fall of Ai was completely different from what happened at Jericho. At Jericho there had been a miracle: the walls had fallen. At Ai there was no miracle. The Israelites had to take the city through the normal processes of war. God is not mechanical but personal. He is not going to deal with every situation in a mechanical way, and we must not reduce him to a series of mechanical acts, as though because God acts one way in one moment he will act the same way in another. We must allow God to be free. God uses many methods. At Jericho there was a miracle; at Ai, none.[19]

Francis A. Schaeffer

My soul, be on thy guard,
    Ten thousand foes arise;
The hosts of sin are pressing hard
    To draw thee from the skies.

Oh, watch, and fight, and pray;
    The battle ne'er give o'er;
Renew it boldly every day
    And help divine implore.

Ne'er think the victory won,
    Nor lay thine armour down.
The work of faith will not be done
    Till thou obtain the crown.

George Heath

Chapter 9

PERILS OF THE PROMISED LAND

The outstanding characteristic of their new homeland, the Hebrews soon discovered, was conflict, but with this difference—it was conflict that issued in victory. Until confronted by the nations of Canaan, they had known little of fighting. True, there had been skirmishes in the desert, but now warfare had begun in grim earnest and on a larger scale—not an isolated battle, but a protracted campaign.

The Christian who supposes that life in the Promised Land is the end of conflict, will soon be disillusioned. Temptations are not fewer but, if anything, more subtle and strong.

The difference now is that in Canaan the battles are fought under the leadership of the Commander of the Lord's hosts who has never known defeat. It is not a life of rest from conflict, but rest in conflict. In their first seven years in Canaan they lost only one battle, and that was due to their culpable sin and disobedience.

In the Christian's Promised Land the believer soon meets spiritual enemies of which he knew little when living the worldly life in the desert. Paul described them in vivid terms:

Our struggle is not against flesh and blood, but against the rulers, against the authorities, against the powers of this dark world and against the spiritual forces of evil in heavenly realms. Therefore put on the full armour of God (Eph 6:12, 13).

Using Old Testament symbolism to illustrate New Testament truth, in Egypt the conflict is with *the world*. In the desert against Amalek, the conflict is with *the flesh*. In Canaan the conflict is with *the devil* and his hosts who strenuously resist the believer's life in the heavenlies and do everything possible to arrest onward progress toward spiritual maturity.

What were the special perils Israel encountered?

The peril of presumption—Ai (Josh 7:1–26)

Ai was a small fortress situated two miles from Jericho but, like that city, it had strategic importance far beyond its size, for it guarded an upper pass, and dominated the Jerusalem road.

Israel had every reason to expect victory. They had a supernatural Leader. They were beneficiaries of the Abrahamic covenant. They had already gained two signal victories at Jordan and Jericho, where God had displayed His might.

Flushed with these successes, they expected an easy victory over little Ai, but they had to learn by bitter experience that victory can be frustrated by disobedience and sin.

The spies who had been sent ahead to reconnoitre, discovered that the army of Ai was small. They recommended that only a token force be dispatched against the city, and Joshua acted on their advice. It was doubtless a justifiable recommendation, but at the end of the day Joshua and the leaders were prone on their faces with dust on their heads and clothes rent, and thirty-six corpses lined the road from Ai. Israel had turned their backs on their enemies.

It looked as though, despite His repeated promises, God had forsaken them. In the light of the tragic facts, what was the value of those promises? They must learn, as we must, that without God the smallest opposition is too much for us.

In his bewilderment and distress Joshua's faith faltered and he gave way to despair. Their enemies would hear of the defeat and their morale would recover! One defeat would lead to another. Joshua moaned:

> O Lord, what can I say now that Israel is routed by its enemies? The Canaanites and the other people of the country will hear about this, and they will surround us and wipe out our name from the earth. What then will you do for your own great name? (Josh 7:8, 9).

A word from the Lord at this time of psychological trauma brought Joshua to his senses:

> Stand up! What are you doing down on your face? Israel has sinned; they have violated my covenant which I commanded them to keep. They have taken some of the devoted things; they have stolen, they have lied, they have put them with their possessions. That is why the Israelites cannot stand against their enemies.... I will not be with you any more unless you destroy whatever among you is devoted to destruction (Josh 7:10–12).

God was saying in effect, 'You speak as though it were I who should act. It is not I, it is you! Stand up! Consecrate the people. Search out the sin and deal with it!' God would not be saddled with the blame for this reverse.

Humiliation and prayer are good and necessary in their place, but they are no substitute for judging and dealing with sin in the life or in the nation. It is very significant that this defeat followed so closely on the heels of glorious victory at the very beginning of a new era in the history of the nation.

It has a New Testament parallel in the judgement that fell on Ananias and Sapphira for a similar sin when the new era of the Church had just commenced (Acts 5:1–10). In both cases God taught a stunning lesson on the seriousness with which He views covetousness and disobedience. He left them in no doubt of the gravity of their actions or of the certainty of judgement.

It is of interest that the word used in the Septuagint Version of the Book of Joshua to describe Achan's sin is the word which is also used to describe the sin of Ananias and Sapphira. They too took a portion of what was devoted to God and their sin brought similar judgement.

Causes of defeat

Before the attack on Jericho was launched, all Israel had concurred in devoting all of the spoils of the city of God. Achan had joined in this agreement. But when he saw the silver and gold and the modish Babylonian garments he was overcome by desire. To use his own words:

'I saw—I coveted—I took—I hid' (6:21).

The same four verbs have since spelt the doom of many another. Gold and silver is always the focus of covetousness. The stylish garment would doubtless appeal to Achan's male pride. It was the badge of modernity and success.

The tragic outcome of his sin seems so out of all proportion to its apparent magnitude, that the incident warrants close analysis.

The causes of their defeat are not far to seek. There was *presumption*, engendered by their spectacular victory at Jericho. Underestimating their enemy, they unilaterally decided to send only a token contingent against them, instead of consulting the Commander. The hour of greatest danger comes when we are flushed with recent victory.

Another contributory factor was *prayerlessness*. Not that Joshua did not pray, but he prayed at the wrong time. Had he made the same preparation before Ai as before Jericho, the story would have been different.

So the failure was not all on the part of Achan. *Joshua failed.* Before the engagement he neglected to consult his Commander-in-Chief and learn His strategy. He acted on the circumstantial evidence and advice of the spies rather than at divine direction.

The spies failed. Their commission was to reconnoitre and report conditions to Joshua, but they assumed the prerogatives of the Commander and dictated strategy.

Achan failed. His seemed a small sin, for he took only a tiny part of the booty. But in its effects it was anything but small. He thought it was a secret sin, locked up in his own heart and his own tent and perhaps within his own family (if they were collaborators). But before long it was public knowledge to the whole nation. Secret sin has public consequences.

There was no outward and obvious connection between the mound of earth in Achan's tent and the thirty-six corpses on the Ai road, and yet they were intimately connected. This was the hidden cause of the demoralization of the whole nation, and the nation was temporarily immobilized because of his secret sin.

> Ah me! the secret sin
> That lurks and works within
> The fair false heart which gives it willing room!
> How sure it bringeth blight,
> Like nipping frost at night
> That withers in the spring its early bloom.
>
> Oh, hidden cherished lust,
> Like a small speck of rust
> On the sheathed sword—known but to God and me;
> What if the weapon good
> Unto the sheath be glued
> On battle-day, and I am shamed by thee?
>
> *Walter C. Smith*

It was wilful sin, for he had received due warning of its seriousness and consequences.

His sin involved others. We cannot sin in isolation. His sin was primarily against God, but also against his family, his tribe and his nation. It brought tragedy to his family, disgrace to his tribe, shame to the nation and dishonour to God. One drop of poison injected into the little finger affects every member of the body.

No action, whether foul or fair,
Is ever done, but it leaves somewhere
A record written by fingers ghostly,
As a blessing or a curse, and mostly
In the greater weakness or the greater strength
Of the acts which will follow it.

Longfellow

Correction of the defeat

God is to be praised that there is no defeat so complete and humiliating that forgiveness, restoration and renewed victory are not possible. No failure need be final. The way in which Israel recovered from its initial reverse and went on to consistent victory, holds great encouragement for us as we wage our battle against sin and Satan, and face our own failures.

The now penitent Joshua speedily placed himself under the Unseen Commander whom he had temporarily ignored. Once again he sought His plan of campaign. Once again with God in command and the sin dealt with, the stage was set for victory. The offender was charged with his offence, and he confessed but that did not save him from judgement.

Varying views of the punishment

There is no unanimity among interpreters of Scripture concerning those who were included in the divine judgement. The passage recording the judgement that was meted out reads:

> Then Joshua, together with all Israel, took Achan, son of Zerah, the silver, the robe, the gold wedge, his sons and daughters, his cattle, donkeys and sheep, his tent and all that he had to the valley of Achor. Joshua said, 'Why

have you brought this disaster on us? The Lord will bring disaster on you today.'

Then all Israel stoned *him*, and after they had stoned the rest, they burned *them*. *Over* Achan they heaped up a large pile of rocks (Josh 7:24–26, italics mine).

There is no doubt about the stoning of Achan, but were all his family stoned and burned with fire? The passage is capable of more than one interpretation. Dr Alfred Edersheim, the great Hebrew Christian scholar, maintains that it does not necessarily follow that his sons and daughters were stoned and burned with him. The plural 'them' of verse 25 could, he says, refer only to the animals and other possessions mentioned in verse 24. The record does not say specifically that his family were stoned, but that all Israel stoned *him*, and the pile of stones was heaped over *him*. The record does not say that his family were implicated, or even that they knew of his action, although it would have been difficult for him to hide the purloined goods in his tent without their knowledge.

If his family did share his fate, it would be because they were implicated in his action and were therefore culpable.

The tragedy of Achan was that had he been content to wait only a few days, he would have had more than he stole, for Israel was permitted to take all the spoil of Ai. Endeavouring to snatch blessings before God's time has arrived can end in tragedy.

The great lesson for us is that though only one person sinned, blessing and victory stopped for all. Sin hinders the advance and the victory of the Church. When we sin in secret, God knows, and blessing slows or stops. We have the option of judging our sin, or having the judgement of God. True repentance and dealing with sin opens the way for renewed blessing.

The peril of compromise—Gibeon (Josh 9:1–27)

If the central lesson of the defeat at Ai is to beware of presumption, the lesson of Israel's involvement with the Gibeonites is to *beware of snares and compromise*.

> Calm seas have their dangers,
> Mariners beware!

Compromise has been defined as 'the endeavour to make the best of incompatibles' (W. G. Scroggie), or the settling of a dispute by making mutual concessions, usually involving a sacrifice of principle. It is a weapon which the Adversary has used with tragic effectiveness in the Church.

Once again Israel is flushed with victory after the rout of the men of Ai. The unchecked onward march of the invaders caused the surrounding nations to pronounce a truce in their inter-tribal warfare and unite against their common foe. So they formed an alliance. Hitherto the people of Israel had faced only single cities, but now they were challenged by a powerful coalition.

However, the wily Gibeonites (who were Hivites) doubted the wisdom of open conflict with Israel. Deciding to resort to subtlety, they adopted a strategy of deception—meeting craft with craft.

They sent ambassadors of peace who professed to have come from a distant country. Their appearance fully substantiated their story—old socks, old wine-skins, tattered garments and shoes, mouldy bread. Today they would be awarded an Oscar for their performance. Joshua and his leaders were suspicious at first, but the visual evidence was so overwhelming! It was here that they made their fatal blunder. 'The men of Israel sampled their provisions, but did not inquire of the Lord' (Josh 9:14).

Satan is far more dangerous in his wiles than in his overt assaults; when he comes as an angel of light than when he attacks as a roaring lion. His assaults are varied and that is why we need the *whole* armour of God. The early Church flourished under the persecutions of Nero but succumbed to the flatteries of Constantine. Joshua had another painful lesson to learn. He had not fully mastered the lesson of Ai.

The story advanced by the Gibeonites was so reasonable and consistent, their references to Jehovah were so reverent, their appearance so in keeping with their claims, that Joshua accepted the circumstantial evidence without first seeking God's mind in prayer. His confidence was in his own good judgement and discernment rather than in God, a mistake still current among the Church's leaders. He made the error of judging 'by what he sees with his eyes' and deciding 'by what he hears with his ears' (Is 11:3). In time of battle we should suspect everything and be alert to detect the Adversary's wiles.

Only three days elapsed before Joshua discovered, to his utter dismay, that these travellers from a distant land were his next-door neighbours! But the discovery came too late—he had already entered into a solemn covenant with them, and God is punctilious in requiring His people to keep faith to their plighted word. In the years that followed the divine prediction was fulfilled, for the Gibeonites were a burden to Joshua and a continual embarrassment to Israel. Compromise with evil always brings trouble and discomfort.

But once again God in mercy overruled Joshua's failure, and brought blessing out of the curse. The Gibeonites became woodcutters and water-carriers (9:23)—cutting wood for the burnt offerings and drawing water for the libations and drink-offerings, as well as for more mundane purposes. Released from these menial tasks, the Israelites were more free to prosecute the warfare against the Canaanites. God frequently allows the results of our compromises to run their natural course, but uses them to serve our spiritual development.

In God's handling of this embarrassing situation, His *grace* shines out. He caused the decpetion of the Gibeonites to bring them into contact with true religion. The city of Gibeon was given to the line of Aaron. David later erected the tabernacle there. In the days of Nehemiah, Gibeonites were numbered among those who rebuilt the walls of Jerusalem.

God's *wisdom* is evidenced in the tasks He assigned to the Gibeonites which were of such a nature as to reduce Israel's contact with these people to a minimum. This greatly lessened the possibility of contagion from their evil practices.

Another illustration of the peril of compromise is afforded by the Ephraimites. The people of Israel *could* have driven the enemy out of their territory, but they chose not to do so. It was much easier to allow them to remain and to draw income from them even though this meant disobeying the command of God. 'They did not dislodge the Canaanites living in Gezer; to this day the Canaanites live among the people of Ephraim but are required to do forced labour' (Josh 16:10).

The dangers inherent in compromise are seen in the fact that the Ephraimites took the lead in practising the idolatry of the Canaanites.

If we have fallen into the snare of compromise, whether wilfully or through ignorance, the door of repentance and restoration is still open. Is it compromise in a business alliance, marriage to an unbeliever, or some other compromising relationship? All is not lost. Let your mistake hew wood and draw water for you Even the memory of our sin can be used to draw us nearer to God. 'God turned the curse into a blessing for you (Deut 23:5).

The peril of indolence

'How long will you wait before you take possession of the land that the Lord, the God of your fathers, has given you?' demanded Joshua (Josh 18:3).

The context makes it clear that the nation had grown war-weary and had succumbed to slothfulness and indolence. They were reluctant to bestir themselves to oust the enemy. Their present conditions were immeasurably better than life in the desert. They had been enriched by the booty from the cities they had captured and things were easy and comfortable. But comfort and affluence are no friends of faith. The people sacrificed future achievement on the altar of present enjoyment. Thus they despised their inheritance and were content to live far below the level of their privilege.

The same temptations beset the Christian in his Promised Land, and he could well pray:

> From subtle love of softening things,
> From easy choices, weakenings,
> From all that dims Thy Calvary,
> O Lamb of God, deliver me.

Amy Wilson Carmichael

Such are some of the representative perils Israel had to face on their Canaan campaign, and which the Christian may expect to meet in his Promised Land.

The battle of Beth-horon—lesson learnt (Josh 10:8)

This battle afforded evidence that Joshua had mastered the lessons of Jericho, Ai and Gibeon. He attacked only when ordered by his Commander. He laid careful plans, for this battle, if won, would bring the whole of Canaan under his control. His surprise attack was wholly successful. He pursued the escaping foe, but saw that they were eluding him. Conscious that God's honour was involved in the battle, Joshua boldly prayed and God answered by prolonging the daylight and sending a devastating hailstorm. Israel was thus enabled to complete the conquest.

Although many victories were achieved, God's ideal for the nation was never fully realized, as the writer of Hebrews commented: 'For if Joshua had given them rest, God would not have spoken later about another day. There remains, then, a Sabbath-rest for the people of God' (Heb 4:8, 9).

Israel perpetually fell just short of the divine ideal for them. Never once did they possess all their inheritance. Never once was the year of Jubilee really observed. The 'rest' they experienced in the land was always temporary. The true rest, 'the rest of faith', awaited the advent of the heavenly Joshua who alone was able to say, 'Come to me and I will give you rest' (Mt 11:28).

The rest of God is no longer relegated to the future but, in response to faith, can be entered upon and enjoyed here and now. 'Therefore, since the promise of entering his rest still stands, let us be careful that none of you be found to have come short of it .... Now we who have believed enter that rest, just as God has said' (Heb 4:1, 3).

> Lord, I believe a rest remains
>   To all Thy people known,
> A rest where pure enjoyment reigns,
>   And Thou art loved alone.
>
> A rest, where all our souls desire
>   Is fixed on things above;
> Where fear and sin and grief expire,
>   Cast out by perfect love.
>
> O, that I now this rest may know,
>   Believe and enter in!
> Now, Saviour, now the power bestow
>   And let me cease from sin.

C. Wesley

PRINCIPLES OF POSSESSION

Joshua 2:1–24; 13:1, 13; 15:63; Exodus 23:27–33;
Numbers 32:1–27

In John's Gospel, 'believe' occurs about fifty times. In every case 'receive' can be substituted with equally good sense. To appropriate is to receive, to take to oneself as one's own.

The central verse of the Bible is reputed to be Psalm 81:10: 'Open wide your mouth and I will fill it.' It pictures a nest of little birds with mouths stretched open beyond belief. Their attitude is the expectation and appropriation of faith. Nor does the mother bird disappoint them....

The wonderful Father in Luke 15 divided his property between his two sons: 'He divided his property between them' (v.12). Despite his glaring faults, the prodigal at least did his father the honour of believing his word and appropriating his share. Not so the elder brother. He even accused his father of not giving him a kid. The deeply hurt father responded: 'Son, all that I have is yours!' Yet he had not appropriated even one kid. The difference was not in bestowal, but in appropriation.

J. O. Sanders

I've reached the land of corn and wine,
And all its riches freely mine;
Here shines undimmed one blissful day,
For all my night has passed away.

My Saviour comes and walks with me,
And sweet communion here have we;
He gently leads me by His hand,
For this is heaven's borderland.

Edgar Page

Chapter 10

PRINCIPLES OF POSSESSION

What can be learned from this epic campaign that will aid us in our spiritual warfare? The principles that were to govern Israel's conduct in their conquest of Canaan are no less applicable to the Christian life.

The principle of reconnaissance (Josh 2:1–24)

Joshua was a prudent military leader. Jericho, guarding as it did the passes into the interior, was the key point in his strategy, so he sent two spies to reconnoitre and bring back a report. 'Go, look over the land, especially Jericho', were his instructions. His purpose in sending them was not to determine whether to attack, but how and when.

But why resort to military strategy at all? The answer is that faith does not respond to God with carelessness. Possession of a divine promise does not mean a relaxation of vigilance. True faith does not despise the employment of appropriate means. To make a promise of God a reason for neglecting prudent precautions is not faith, but presumption.

The two spies crossed the Jordan and slipped into

Jericho, but that fortress had its own security system and their surreptitious entry was soon discovered. That, in the providence of God, they chose Rahab's house proved fortuitous both for her and for them.

Rahab, the central figure in the drama, played a significant part in the campaign. She was both a prostitute and an accomplished liar, but in this unpromising life God discerned true faith, the one quality without which it is impossible to please God.

The question naturally arises, 'Was Rahab's lying justifiable under the circumstances?' Can lying ever be justified? Does the end justify the means? Situational ethics would maintain that a lie might be justified in certain situations—a position that would leave us with no absolute standard of truth. Who is to be the judge?

In this connection it should be remembered that Rahab had been reared among a degenerate people to whom lying and immorality were routine. She saw lying as a choice between two evils. According to oriental ethics, guarding the life of one's guest was an act of hospitality. It was one of the highest virtues. But God did not need her lies. He could have preserved the spies in a dozen other ways.

The testimony of Scripture is consistent—all lies are sinful and sin is never sanctioned by God who exhorts us to 'put off falsehood and speak truthfully' (Eph 4:25).

James mentions Rahab favourably: 'In the same way, was not even Rahab the prostitute considered righteous for what she did when she gave lodging to the spies and sent them off in a different direction?' (Jas 2:25). But what was it for which she was commended?

In acting as she did, Rahab was taking her life in her hands. She had to choose between loyalty to her nation and loyalty to her newly-discovered God. Had her deception been discovered, her life would not have been worth a moment's purchase. It was her bravery and unselfish action that James commends, not her lies and deception.

The information that Rahab gave the spies concerning the morale of the Canaanites greatly encouraged Joshua. 'I know that the Lord has given this land to you and that a great fear of you has fallen on us, so that all who live in this country are melting in fear because of you' (Josh 2:9). She confessed her confidence in the God of Israel: 'The Lord your God is God in heaven above and on the earth below' (Josh 2:11).

All the other inhabitants of Canaan possessed the same knowledge of God's dealings with Israel as Rahab and had the same opportunity for repentance, but it did not lead them to faith. Rahab alone believed, asked for mercy and received it. Though surrounded by a hostile environment, she exercised faith in a God who was the antithesis of the gods she had worshipped.

What a commentary on the mercy and grace of God that she should become a member of the true Israel, marry a prince of Judah, become a progenitor of the Messiah and find her place among the heroes of faith in God's Roll of Honour in Hebrews 11!

The believer, too, is enjoined to engage in reconnaissance, to be alert to the strategy of the Adversary. 'Be self-controlled and alert. Your enemy the devil prowls around like a lion looking for someone to devour' (1 Pet 5:8).

The principle of dispossession

Co-existence with the nations of Canaan was expressly forbidden. But before Israel could possess the land with its cities and houses, they must dispossess the present inhabitants and this meant stern conflict. 'I will hand over to you the people who live in the land and you will drive them out before you' (Ex 23:31), was the divine promise. But failure to dispossess them would involve Israel in endless trouble, as they proved to their cost. 'If you do not drive out the inhabitants of the land, those you allow to remain will become barbs in your eyes and thorns in your sides. They will give you trouble in the land where you will live' (Num 33:55). No quarter was to be given.

We each have in embryo in our hearts the equivalent of the seven nations of Canaan. Jesus gave an unflattering diagnosis:

> From within, out of men's hearts, come evil thoughts, sexual immorality, theft, murder, adultery, greed, malice, deceit, lewdness, envy, slander, arrogance and folly. All these evils come from inside and make a man 'unclean' (Mk 7:21–23).

If we give quarter and house-room to these sins and do not avail ourselves of the mighty victory gained for us by our Lord on Calvary, our experience will be like that of the unbelieving Israelites. 'Put off your old self which is being corrupted by its deceitful desires', is the divine commandment (Eph 4:22).

But is not this something beyond our powers? Have many of us not tried and failed a hundred times?

Perhaps these sins seem more firmly entrenched than ever? The good news is that we are not left to do this alone and unaided. Here is His promise to Israel and to us: 'My angel will go ahead of you and bring you into the land of the Amorites, Hittites...and I will wipe them out' (Ex 23:23). Israel was His instrument, but God supplied the dynamic for the achievement of His purposes. In the event, Israel possessed only as much of the land as they dispossessed.

The principle of appropriation
(Josh 1:3; Eph 1:3; 2 Pet 1:3)

This principle has been mentioned earlier, but it is appropriate to consider it further in this context, for it is one of the vital secrets of the Christian life. Thousands who lived drab, defeated lives have experienced a radical transformation through mastering the art of appropriation, of turning promises into facts, of making their own in experience what God has given them.

The land had been given, but every square foot had to be personally possessed. The cities were already there, but they must be occupied. The houses were built, but they must be lived in. So is it with the broad land of God's promises.

On some farms there is a patent cattle-trough designed to supply fresh water to the cattle as they require it and at the same time to obviate waste in time of drought.

The trough is built in the centre of a platform under which is a strong steel spring. When the animal treads on the platform, the spring is compressed and this opens a valve which allows the water to flow freely into the trough. So, as long as the animal remains on the platform, just so long will the water flow. When it moves away, the valve closes and the flow of water ceases. The supply of water is always there but it is apparent only when appropriated.

God has made available to us the unsearchable riches of Christ, a limitless supply always available, but only that on which we place our feet becomes ours in actuality.

Peter makes a tremendous assertion in 2 Peter 1:3: 'His divine power has given us everything we need for life and godliness through our knowledge of him who called us by his own glory and goodness.' Taken at its face value, this means that there is nothing we will ever need to enable us to live a holy and victorious life which has not become ours by virtue of our union with Christ. But unless we plant the foot of faith on these blessings, we are none the better for their bestowal.

William Penn, from whom the State of Pennsylvania takes its name, so befriended and ingratiated himself with the Red Indians of that State that they made a gift to him of all the land he could walk around in a day. Taking them at their word, Penn rose early the next morning and walked briskly all day until dusk. When he returned to the camp at twilight one of the Indian chiefs quizzically said, 'The paleface has had a very long walk today!' But they were not displeased. He had honoured their word, and they honoured his trust. The land he encircled that day is now the city of Philadelphia.

Surely we should not have less trust in our faithful God? When we claim the blessings He assures us He has bestowed, He will be as good as our faith. No amount of power or willingness on the part of God can make up for lack of trust on ours.

The principle of progression (Ex 23:29, 30; Deut 7:22)

The Israelites were not required to possess the whole land at once. 'The Lord your God will drive out those nations before you, *little by little.* You will not be allowed to eliminate them all at once, or the wild animals will multiply around you' (Deut 7:22, italics mine).

At first blush it would have seemed better if the nations were expelled or exterminated all at once; or at least quickly. But God knew that the people of Israel were too few to effectively control the wild beasts, so He said 'I will not drive them out in a single year, because the land would become desolate.... Little by little I will drive them out before you, until you have increased enough to take possession of the land' (Ex 23:29, 30). God is realistic in His expectations.

The work of sanctification in the life of the believer is also progressive. There are stages of spiritual growth. We are not expected to attain overnight to the degree of holiness reached by a John Wesley or a Murray McCheyne, but we are expected to 'go on to maturity' (Heb 6:1). The promise of possession of the land was for one step at a time.

To the very end there will remain unexplored territory in our lives to be subdued and brought under the sway of our Master. The crisis of sanctification leads to a never-ending process that will be consummated only when we see Him and are like Him (1 Jn 3:2). Growth in grace is not instantaneous like regeneration, and this should keep us in a state of constant dependence on the Lord who will increase the area of our victory as we are ready to experience it.

Let no one think that sudden in a minute
All is accomplished, and the work is done.
Though in thy earliest dawn thou shouldst begin it,
Scarce were it ended in thy setting sun.

F. W. H. Myers

The principle of renunciation (Deut 7:2)

The Hebrews were leaving behind for ever the bondage of Canaan, and entering a new land that demanded a new life. The twelve stones left in the bed of the Jordan to be overwhelmed by the returning waters (Josh 4:9 margin) symbolized that the Old Israel was dead, and the new cairn erected on the Canaan side of Jordan proclaimed that they were a renewed people. As Paul put it, they had come through death to newness of life. The old life of Egypt with its bondage and corrupting influences was behind them for ever. The returning waters of the Jordan separated them from the old life. What point would there be in destroying the evils of Canaan if the evils of Egypt had been allowed to penetrate?

The renunciation of Egypt was to be complete and final, and no new treaties were to be made with the people of Canaan. 'When you have defeated them, then you must destroy them totally. Make no treaty with them' (Deut 7:2).

The Christian is enjoined to reckon himself, to count

THE CHRISTIAN'S PROMISED LAND

himself 'dead to sin but alive to God in Christ Jesus' (Rom 6:11). Allowing elements of the old life to remain will only retard spiritual progress. A worldly Christian whose standards have been lowered to meet the compromising conditions of his environment, can never exercise the qualities of salt and light in this corrupt world. In order to make a spiritual impact on our generation, we must be set free from the adverse influences of both Egypt and Canaan by an act of irrevocable renunciation.

Partial possession

As He had promised, God led his people to victory in many battles until the power of the nations of Canaan was effectively, though not completely, broken. But the record of these remarkable conquests was marred by the melancholy refrain:

> But the Israelites did not drive out the people of Geshur and Maacah, so they continue to live among the Israelites to this day (Josh 13:13).

> Judah could not dislodge the Jebusites, who were living in Jerusalem; to this day the Jebusites live there with the people of Judah (Josh 15:63).

> The Manassites were not able to occupy these towns, for the Canaanites were determined to live in that region (Josh 17:12).

> When Joshua was old and well advanced in years, the Lord said to him, 'You are very old, and there are still large areas of land to be taken over' (Josh 13:1).

It proved a disastrous mistake to have allowed the nations to remain in their midst through a failure of faith and endeavour. We make a similar mistake and experience similar problems when we fail to assert our share in the victory of Calvary over the sins and failures in our lives. Behind the assurance, 'Sin shall not be your master' (Rom 6:14), lies all the power of the risen Christ.

In the light of the magnitude of God's gift to Israel, and the resources He placed at their disposal, it is pathetic that they never enjoyed their full inheritance.

Our spiritual charter, too, is much wider than our actual wealth. We receive pardon and forgiveness, and too often are content with that, instead of pressing on to enjoy all the privileges of joint-heirship with Christ. While revelling in the assurance of their justification, too many Christians fail to press on to an experience of practical and progressive sanctification.

Let us cultivate a holy discontent and not be satisfied with partial possession of our spiritual inheritance.

Non-possession (Num 32:5, 7; 7:16–37)

Israel's partial possession of their inheritance was bad enough, but the tribes of Reuben, Gad and Manasseh succumbed to an even worse peril and came even further short of the divine ideal.

Even after the signal victories they had seen, these tribes were content to rest just short of the Promised Land—near, but not in it. They had pressed Moses to grant them the delectable pastoral land they had selected on the desert side of Jordan (Josh 1:12–15). Moses acceded to their request, but only after they had consented to fight alongside the other tribes until Canaan was subdued (Num 32:5–7, 16–37).

At first sight that seemed quite a satisfactory course. They risked their lives with their brethren. But that did not alter the fact that they had chosen the land that bordered on Egypt, not Canaan. They find their counterpart today in those who believe there is a life of blessing and fulfilment, but choose to live nearer the world with which they have more affinity.

Many Christians travel a long way towards Canaan, come to the very boundary, but the demands of full surrender and obedience are too stringent. Life in the Christian's Promised Land would involve too much renunciation and self-denial. Sheltered by the blood of Christ, they have crossed the Red Sea and traversed the desert. They have even sampled the fruit of the land, but they are not prepared for the step of faith that will bring them safely across Jordan and into permanent residence in Canaan. The temptation to settle just short of Canaan proves too strong.

The history of these border-dwellers affords a serious warning to those facing the same temptation. They were the first to fall before the invading Assyrians and were swept into a captivity from which they never returned. Ever after they were a source of trouble and embarrassment to the Israelites. They became like two separate nations, having different dialects and frequent disagreements. A border-dweller can always be detected by his dialect! He does not speak the pure language of Canaan.

Who were their descendants? The Gadarenes who 'asked Jesus to leave them because they were overcome with fear', when the herd of pigs rushed into the sea and were drowned (Lk 8:37).

The contemporary lesson is that we choose the level on which we live our Christian lives. God did not compel the two and a half tribes to cross the Jordan. They made their choice and He ratified it. Nor does He force His blessings on us. If we prefer not to take the decisive step, we are left with the consequences. It is recorded of Israel that 'He gave them what they asked for, but sent a wasting disease among them' (Ps 106:15).

AN OPTIMISTIC VIEW OF OLD AGE

Joshua 14:6–13; 15:14–19

Caleb followed the Lord wholly through the weary years in the wilderness. Amid the marchings and counter-marchings, the innumerable deaths, the murmurings and rebellions of the people, he retained a steadfast purpose to do only God's will, to please Him, to know no other leader, and to heed no other voice.

It was of no use to try and involve that stout lion's whelp, for that is the underlying thought in his name, in any movement against Moses and Aaron. He would be no party to Miriam's spite. He would not be allured by the wiles of the girls of Moab. Always strong, and pure, and true and noble; like a rock in a changeful sea; like a snowcapped peak amid the change of cloud, and storm and sun. A man in whose strong nature weaker natures could hide; and who must have been a tower of strength to that new and young generation which grew up to fill the vacant places in the van of Israel.[20]

F. B. Meyer

There is a foe whose hidden power
    The Christian well may fear,
More subtle far than inbred sin
    And to the heart more dear.
It is the power of selfishness,
    It is the wilful I,

And e'er my Lord can live in me
   My very self must die.

There is like Anak's sons of old
   A race of giants still
Self-glorifying, self-confidence,
   Self-seeking and self-will.
Still must these mighty Anakim
   By Caleb's sword be slain,
E'er Hebron's heights of heavenly love
   Of conquering feet can gain.

A. B. Simpson

Chapter 11

AN OPTIMISTIC VIEW OF OLD AGE

Canaan had been largely subdued. The coalitions of the Canaanite nations had been smashed. The time had arrived to distribute the territory among the war-weary tribes so that they could enter in and enjoy their inheritance.

The first to claim his inheritance was Joshua's faithful colleague, Caleb. His father, Jephunneh, was a Kenezite, an Edomite who traced his descent through Eliphaz, Esau's eldest son (Gen 36:11). He apparently joined the tribe of Judah and married the daughter of Hur, through whom Caleb inherited the prerogatives of her clan.

The fact that he was a foreigner who broke 'his birth's invidious bar', emphasized the fact that God's purposes went far beyond the bounds of Israel. *Smith's Dictionary* speaks of him as 'one of the first fruits of the Gentile harvest of which Jethro, Rahab, Ruth, Naaman and many others were samples and signs.'

The name Caleb means 'all heart', and he proved to be a worthy Old Testament counterpart of John Bunyan's 'Mr Greatheart'. His chief distinction lay in the fact that he never stopped growing. The passing of the years, instead of witnessing his gradual eclipse, only served to increase his stature and enhance his prestige. His name is appropriately derived from a Hebrew word associated with the ideas of fidelity, obedience and alertness to discern his master's will—qualities in which he excelled.

His biography, which is condensed into a few sentences, illustrates two exhilarating truths. One, that it is possible for *life's greatest achievement* to take place in old age. The other, that there is *no retiring age* in the service of God. At no stage of life does he disappoint our highest expectations.

Like Moses, his life divides into three clearly defined periods. Until the age of forty, he was a slave in Egypt. Then, as a leader in his tribe, he was selected as one of twelve to explore Canaan, and thereafter spent a second forty years in the desert. It was in the third period of his life that he accomplished his greatest achievement.

Zealous in youth

His first mention in Scripture (Num 13:6) is as a comparatively young man. His early life is not recorded, but from his subsequent history we are afforded insight into his character and conduct while a young man. The clue is found in Numbers 13:1, when the Lord said to Moses, 'Send some men to explore the land of Canaan which I am giving to the Israelites. From each ancestral tribe, send *one of its leaders*.' That tells its own story. Leaders do not just happen. Behind the scenes there has been strong discipline and sterling character. Of our Lord's thirty years of obscurity, only one incident is recorded, but the subsequent years of holy living and selfless service tell us all we need to know about His youth.

The crisis *reveals* the man, it does not make him. Until the crisis of the shipwreck (Acts 27:1), Paul was just one of 'certain other prisoners' (AV). But when the crisis arose he became undisputed master of the situation.

The crisis for Caleb came with his selection to explore Canaan. His character and native gifts won for him a place in the leadership of his tribe and nation. He was never numbered among the murmurers, nor did he hanker for the lost delicacies of Egypt. His goal was the Promised Land and he allowed nothing to deflect him.

Of many admirable qualities, two stand out conspicuously.

He displayed great courage

His *moral courage* was highlighted when he and Joshua stood alone against the swiftly-flowing tide of popular opinion. It takes a strong man or woman to stand alone and this is one of the most stringent tests for young people, who naturally crave popularity. Peer pressure can be an awesome thing and it is sometimes agonizing to oppose a course when 'everyone is doing it'. It is all too easy to maintain a guilty silence in an adverse theological climate.

It took no small degree of *physical courage* to maintain his attitude of faith and opposition to the popular majority report of the ten spies, when 'the whole assembly talked about stoning them' (Num 14:10).

But Caleb refused to be intimidated and do violence to his convictions even to save his life. He was willing to hazard all for God.

*He evidenced a robust and unwavering faith
in unpropitious circumstances*

This is a quality that ranks high in God's scale of values, since 'without faith it is impossible to please God' (Heb 11:6). His faith was the more remarkable because it flourished luxuriantly among the miasmas of unbelief arising from the pessimistic majority report:

> The people who live there are powerful, and
> the cities are fortified and very large.
> We even saw descendants of Anak (giants) there.
> We can't attack those people; they are stronger
>   than we are.
> The land we explored devours those living in it.
> All the people we saw there are of great size.
> We seemed like grasshoppers in our own eyes.
>   (Num 13:28, 31–33)

Can you not feel the temperature falling with every sentence of the report? It was into this chilling atmosphere that Caleb injected a shot of faith. A comparison of his report with that of the Timorous Ten is almost ludicrous in its optimism:

> Then Caleb silenced the people before Moses and said,
>   'We should go up and take possession of the land.
>   We can certainly do it.
>   The land we passed through and explored is exceedingly good,
>   A land flowing with milk and honey.

139

Do not be afraid of the people of the land.
We will swallow them up.
Their protection is gone.
The Lord is with us.
Do not be afraid of them.'
(Num 13:30; 14:7–9)

But, alas, this magnificent blending of faith and courage failed to elicit a positive response from the people. Caleb and Joshua had seen all the Ten had seen. They had neither underestimated the power of their foes, nor minimized the size of the task before them. The difference of outlook lay in the fact that the Ten matched the strength of the giants with their grasshopper strength and were demoralized, while the Two matched it against the omnipotence of God. The Ten gazed at the giants, Caleb and Joshua gazed at God and this was the source of their confidence.

Difficulties dwindled before their virile faith. Were there fearsome giants in the land? They were bread for them, and as one writer quaintly put it, 'The bigger the giant, the bigger the loaf.' They saw and trusted a God infinitely greater then the giants. Faith imparts true perspective.

Unbelief has a notoriously short memory. The Ten urged the people, 'We should choose a leader and go back to Egypt' (Num 14:4). How soon they had forgotten the taskmaster's lash and the bitterness of the slavery from which they had been delivered—which is a parable! But for Caleb there was no going back, only forward. He countered their fear and unbelief with his confident, 'Let us go up.'

Consistent in mid-life

In a recent news report there was an item with the caption, 'Middle Age—the Best of Times?' The writer pointed out that the apparent security of middle-aged Americans is being shaken on several fronts—divorce, financial worries, job-loss—and they feel the American economy has betrayed them; the American dream has turned sour.

Mid-life has its own *peculiar testings* in both physical and spiritual realms. They may not be so volcanic as those of youth, but what they lose in intensity they gain in subtlety. Many who soared like rockets in their youth have descended like burnt-out sticks in middle age. Marriage has knocked many a young man and woman out of active spiritual warfare.

There are usually *obvious advantages* when we attain this stage of life. Our powers are at their zenith. Important life-decisions—career, friends, marriage, family—have been made. Ideally, status and influence have been attained, and financial circumstances are somewhat easier. We now know many of the answers to the problems we face and can be more objective in our views.

But there are *counter-balancing dangers*. It is often at this stage of life that there develops a loss of fervour and a waning of personal devotion. A lukewarm sense of duty replaces ardent heart love. Instead of transmuting the vanishing enthusiasms of youth into a worthy and absorbing life-purpose, life becomes insipid and anaemic. The temptation to ease up on self-denial and yield to softening ease is weakly succumbed to. It is at this period in life we would do well to pray:

> God, harden me against myself,
>> The coward with pathetic voice
>> Who craves for ease and rest and joy.
> Myself, arch-traitor to myself,
>> My hollowest friend,
>> My deadliest foe,
>> My clog, whatever road I go.

Amy Wilson Carmichael

Often unrealized ideals of marriage and home-life are condoned and accepted as inevitable. With the fixing of life's tendencies and habits, disillusionment and even cynicism become the pattern of life. All unconsciously a subtle deterioration sets in. As the Lord said of Ephraim, 'His hair is sprinkled with gray, but he does not notice' (Hos 7:9). It is very easy to stop growing and striving after greater spiritual maturity and feel we have earned the right to indulge ourselves.

As we saw, Caleb passed the tests of youth with flying colours, but how will he fare in the heavier and long drawn-out tests of mid-life? Gordon Chilvers maintained that in middle life we need the resources of God more than we ever needed them before or are likely to need them again. Did Caleb draw on these resources?

Few have faced so hard and embittering a lot as he. The sin and unbelief of his contemporaries doomed him to a life of frustration and disappointment for the forty years that should have been the best of his life. The apparent reward of his faith and courage was aimless trekking in a barren desert when his powers were at their peak. There were funerals every day.

By all worldly standards Caleb would have been justified in being petulant and resentful, but he maintained his spiritual integrity and survived the long-sustained test without losing stature. He was one of the rare souls who was not offended with God in His inscrutable dealings with him.

When Moses died, it was Joshua, not Caleb who was chosen by God to be Israel's leader. But in this great man's heart there was neither jealousy of Joshua nor resentment against God. He loyally and willingly served in the inferior office. One writer says:

> The hardest part of the journey is the middle mile. There is the enthusiasm of the new undertaking which buoys at the start, the thrill of reaching the goal at the finish. But it is the middle mile when you are a long way from the start and home is still distant, that tests the mettle of the runner. On the middle mile of life's pilgrimage, the believer needs most the grace of patient continuance.[21]

In his youth Caleb soared with wings as an eagle. Now he has mastered the art of running without wearying, stabilized by the vitality of his faith. But can he walk without fainting in old age?

Adventurous in old age

No other Bible character presents such an inspiring and optimistic conception of old age. The supreme challenge of his life came when he was eighty-five years old, the age when most are dreaming only of security and comfortable retirement. But Caleb, the hero of forty, is no less a hero at eighty-five. He demonstrated that old age, which is commonly viewed as a tragedy, can be turned into glorious achievement.

William Barclay told of receiving a letter which concluded with, 'Yours, eighty-three years old and still growing'—another Caleb. To him old age was not petering out, but pressing on to grander attainments; not slowly descending the mountain, but scaling another peak; not senility, but adventure and achievement. His life moved steadily forward, not to termination merely, but to consummation.

At every stage of life he towered above his contemporaries. In youth he stood alone. In mid-life he walked alone. In old age he climbed alone.

> For age is opportunity no less
> Than youth itself, though in another dress.
> And as the evening twilight fades away
> The sky is filled with stars, invisible by day.

H. W. Longfellow

For forty-five years Caleb had patiently waited for the fulfilment of God's promise to him through Moses (Josh 14:9). In his interview with Joshua at the partitioning of the land he referred five times to the promise which through the weary desert years had buoyed him up as the guarantee of possession of his inheritance in Canaan. The passing years had done nothing to quench his faith in God, or to dampen his ardent spirit. J. Russell Howden wrote:

144

Faith enables a man to take long views. It lifts him out of the ephemeral and temporary into the eternal and permanent. It corrects his perspective because it sees eternity on the horizon.

Caleb's faith in the far-off promise was nourished by daily instalments of fulfilment, for he had received two promises—one that his life should be prolonged, the other that he should receive the district into which he had ventured (Num 14:30). The daily fulfilment of the first was a continual pledge of the second.[23]

He was spiritually virile

'I am still as strong today as the day Moses sent me out. I'm just as vigorous to go out to battle now as I was then' (Josh 14:22). Few octogenarians are so fortunate as he! But it must be borne in mind that his victory was one of *the spirit*, not of the body.

Paul did not have such physical youthfulness in later years, for at sixty or less, he described himself as 'Paul the aged'. But to the last he was young in intellect and spirit. Not all are blessed with such physical health, but all can be strong in spirit. This old man who should have been pulling on his slippers was talking of binding on shoes of iron, so that he could ascend the mountain and rout the giants before whom the Timorous Ten had quailed.

He was spiritually audacious

'Now give me this hill-country (Mountain, KJV) that the Lord promised me that day' was his request—not fertile river flat or easy places, but the mountain which held the fearsome giants. He asked for the most difficult assignment of all! His request revealed the calibre of the man. How different an attitude to that of a young prospective missionary who asked his Board to assign him to a place where the Communists would not come! The flame of Caleb's courage had not died down even in old age.

He made his request with his eyes wide open. Had God not stated that He had given Israel every place that the sole of their feet should tread upon? (Josh 1:3). What mountain had Caleb's feet trodden? Hebron, the most powerful stronghold of the enemy (Num 13:21, 22)!

Hebron, a strategic city in the hill country, was probably the choicest spot in the land—fertile, highly elevated, with a wonderful view. To Caleb it was sacred soil, for it was there that the patriarchs had spent most of their lives. Beneath its oaks Abraham had pitched his tents. Its soil had been trodden by the Son of God when He visited those tents. There Abraham and Sarah, Isaac and Rebekah, Jacob and Leah lay buried.

Caleb would be content with nothing less than the best of the land, even though it involved dangerous conflict. Most are content with the good. Only a few are prepared to pay the price for the best, for God's best gifts are the most costly. Satan disputes our way most fiercely, not on the plains of average blessing but on the heights.

Caleb's ambitious request, '*Give me this mountain*', is a grand watchword for the ageing Christian. As we near old age, do we lose the spirit of adventure and aggression, become hesitant to risk another step of faith for God? Do we shrink from the rigours of battle? Perhaps we, too, should remove our slippers and attack some menacing mountain in which the enemies of God are entrenched.

> Make me Thy happy mountaineer,
>   O God most high;
> My climbing soul would welcome the austere:
>   Lord, crucify
> On rock or scree, ice-cliff or field of snow,
> The softness that would sink to things below.
>
> Make us thy mountaineers:
> We would not linger on the lower slope,
> Fill us afresh with hope, Thou God of hope,
> That undefeated we may climb the hill
>   As seeing Him who is invisible.

Amy Wilson Carmichael

Caleb is an endless source of encouragement and inspiration. The message of his life is, '*The best is yet to be.*' He never ceased growing because his devotion to God never weakened.

'Marvellous old man,' wrote Dinsdale Young. 'Effervescent with youthfulness at eighty-five! Jubilant in prospect of driving out the Anakim! Caleb has youth's strength and valour and optimism even in old age.'[24]

Remarkable achievements in old age have not been confined to ancient days. The late Canon C. H. Nash who founded what is now the Bible College of Victoria, Australia, and trained a thousand young men and women for Christian service, retired from the Principalship at the age of seventy. When he was eighty, he received an assurance from the Lord that a further fruitful ministry of ten years lay ahead of him. This assurance was abundantly realized. During those years he was uniquely blessed in a Bible teaching ministry to key groups of clergy and laymen. It was his opinion that these were probably the most fruitful years of his life. When he was ninety, I found him just finishing the sixth volume of Toynbee's monumental history. Like Caleb, he defied the natural order and continued to increase in stature right to the very end.

Benjamin Ririe retired as a missionary of the China Inland Mission when he reached the age of seventy. When he was eighty and found time hanging on his hands, he decided to learn New Testament Greek, as he had lacked the opportunity when he was younger. He became proficient in reading the Greek New Testament. At ninety years of age he attended a refresher course in Greek at a Toronto Theological Seminary. When he was a hundred years old, he was present at a meeting at which I was speaking. In his pocket was a small, well-worn Greek Lexicon which he used to brush up his Greek as he travelled on the subway to and from the meeting! He was in the true succession of Caleb.

One of the most striking aspects of Caleb's triumph was that while none of the younger men of Israel—all his own contemporaries had fallen in the desert—succeeded in totally expelling the enemy from their territory, he completely routed the enemy from his area, including even the giants, for it is recorded that 'from Hebron Caleb drove out the three Anakites—Sheshai, Ahiman and Talmai—descendants of Anak' (Josh 15:14).

Concerning the other Israelites among whom the land was apportioned, there runs the melancholy refrain, 'They did not utterly drive them out... The Canaanites would dwell in the land.... There are still very large areas of land to be taken over.'

Two reasons are assigned for this failure to dislodge and dispossess their foes. First, *sheer inability*. 'The Manassites were not able to occupy these towns, for the Canaanites were determined to live in that region' (Josh 17:12). Lack of faith gave rise to a lack of conquering power. Second, *slackness and indolence*. 'How long will you wait before you begin to take possession of the land that the God of your fathers has given you?' Joshua chided them (Josh 18:3). The Christian warrior can succumb to the same discouragements.

Caleb had a genius for encouragement and our discouraged world stands in dire need of such optimistic warriors. We must not let age dull our hopefulness. Dr Johnson used to say, 'We old fellows must not go discouraging one another.'

Caleb's Secret

What was the secret that enabled Caleb to succeed while the younger Israelites failed? It was enshrined in seven words: '*I followed the Lord my God wholeheartedly.*' The importance of his secret is underscored by the number of times it is reiterated. His undivided allegiance to the Lord was never withdrawn. Dinsdale Young says that the figure behind the original expression is nautical. The idea is of a ship in full sail: a vessel which goes straight on. There had been no divergences, no swerving from a direct course.[22]

'*I followed the Lord my God wholeheartedly*', Caleb was able to testify with a clear conscience. This was not proud boasting but a plain statement of an undeflected aim.

'*You have followed the Lord my God wholeheartedly,*' Moses was able to add in testimony (Josh 14:9). As leader of the nation, Moses had every opportunity of appraising Caleb's character and devotion to God.

But the most astounding testimony comes from God Himself: '*My servant Caleb has a different spirit and follows me wholeheartedly*' (Num 14:24). What higher eulogy could have been made?

The conclusion is plain and the lesson obvious. Caleb completely subdued and dispossessed his enemies, giants and all, because he followed the Lord wholeheartedly. He entertained no divided loyalties. Throughout his life there was consistent obedience to light received, and uncomplaining acceptance of God's will.

Although God moved slowly to fulfil His promise, Caleb was content to wait His time. In New Testament language, he presented his body a living sacrifice to God as a logical act of worship (Rom 12:1), in striking contrast to the faithless multitude whose bodies fell in the desert because they were unwilling to make that sacrifice.

So Caleb dwelt in Hebron, the place of fellowship and communion with God, the very place where God had given Abraham the promise of the Land. 'Then the land had rest from war.'

There are lessons of permanent value to be gained,

* The person who follows the Lord wholeheartedly will grow increasingly like Him in character and outlook.

* Following the Lord wholly involves a call to sacrificial service.

* Laying claim to our inheritance will involve us in new conflict.

* Consistent obedience, though often costly, increases moral strength for further conflict and obedience.

* Fidelity to God's commands enriches the whole life.

From Caleb, too, we learn that faith is contagious and can be emulated by members of one's family. After Caleb had driven the giants out of Hebron:

From there he marched against the people living in Debir (formerly called Kiriath Sepher). And Caleb said, 'I will give my daughter Acsah in marriage to the man who attacks and captures Kiriath-Sepher.' Othniel son of Kenaz, Caleb's brother, took it; so Caleb gave his daughter Acsah to him in marriage (Josh 15:15–17).

Caleb had given his daughter some land in the Negev as a dowry. But Acsah was not satisfied. What was the use of land in a country of that nature if it was not supplied with adequate water? So during the marriage celebrations she spoke to her father:

'Do me a special favour. Since you have given me land in the Negev, give me also springs of water.' So Caleb gave her the upper and lower springs (Josh 15:18, 19).

> 'You have given...'
> 'Give me also...'
> 'And he gave...'

Acsah's father delighted in responding to his daughter's request. He expected great things from God and he obtained them. Acsah expected great things from her father and she was not disappointed.

God is pleased with the spiritual ambition that would make use of the above cheering formula in our approach to Him in prayer.

Do we find our title much larger then the spiritual territory we actually occupy and enjoy? In our lives are there still enemies that refuse to budge, giants who laugh at our puny efforts to dislodge them. If so, there is a reason.

It could be that we have failed to appropriate our inheritance. Or there could be some inner reservation, something that short-circuits spiritual power and saps vitality. Caleb's secret is open to us. Complete victory comes from restful confidence and unreserved obedience.

Those of us who are ageing will find these lines from Longfellow's *Morituri salutamis* stimulating:

> It is too late! Ah, nothing is too late
> Till the tired heart shall cease to palpitate.
> Cato learned Greek at eighty; Sophocles
> Wrote his grand Oedipus, and Simondes
> Bore off the prize of verse from his compeers
> When each had numbered more than four-score years;
> And Theophrastus, at fourscore and ten,
> Had but begun his 'Characters of men'.
> Chaucer at Woodstock, with the nightingales,

At sixty wrote the Canterbury Tales.
Goeth at Weimar, toiling to the last,
Completed Faust when eighty years were past.

What then? Shall we sit idly down and say
The night hath come; it is no longer day?

For age is opportunity, no less
Than youth itself, though in another dress.
And as the evening twilight fades away
The night is filled with stars, invisible by day.

NOTES

1. George A. Turner, *A New and Living Way* (Minneapolis: Bethany Fellowship, 1975), p.77.
2. Major General O. O. Howard, 'Joshua's Genius for Military Leadership', *The Sunday School Times*, 21 September, 1907, p.475.
3. Clarence E. Macartney, *The Greatest Men of the Bible* (Nashville, Abungdon Cokesbury, 1941), p.204.
4. W. S. Hooton, *The Destruction of the Canaanites*, in *The Life of Faith*, 23 February 1938, p.176.
5. Francis A. Schaeffer, *Joshua and the Flow of Biblical History*, (Downers Grove, Ill., Inter-Varsity Press, 1975), p.68.
6. A. Rendle Short, in *Life of Faith*, 23 February, 1938, p.176.
7. Colin C. Kerr, *The Christian's Promised Land*, in the *Keswick Week*, 1937 (London, Marshall Morgan & Scott), p.177.
8. Alexander Maclaren, *Expositions of Holy Scripture—Numbers*, (New York, G. H. Doran Co., no date), p.340.
9. Quoted in J. Sidlow Baxter, *Explore the Book*, Vol. 1 (London, Marshall Morgan & Scott, 1951), p.250.
10. Jessie Penn-Lewis, *The Conquest of Canaan*, (Bournemouth, Overcomer Trust, 1911), p.12.

11. G. F. Maclear, *Cambridge Bible, Book of Joshua* (Cambridge, University Press, 1883), p.45.

12. W. Graham Scroggie, *Land of Life and Rest,* (Glasgow, Pickering & Inglis).

13. In *Zondervan's Pictorial Bible Dictionary,* Article, 'Jericho', (Grand Rapids, Zondervan Publishing House, 1951), p.413.

14. R. W. Kirby in *The Reaper,* June 1970, p.182.

15. J. Hudson Taylor, *The Fire Burns On* (London, OMF Publishers, 1965), p.19.

16. Paul E. Toms, *This Land is Your Land,* (Glendale, Gospel Light Publications, 1977), p.170.

17. J. Russell Howden in *Sunday School Times,* 23 October 1926, p.620.

18. J. J. Davis, *Conquest and Crisis* (Grand Rapids, Baker, 1969), p.53.

19. Francis A. Schaeffer, *Joshua and the Flow of Biblical History* (Downers Grove, Inter-Varsity Press, 1975), p.112.

20. Frederick B. Meyer, *Joshua* (London, Morgan & Scott, 1922), pp.144, 145.

21. J. Russell Howden in *The Sunday School Times,* 30 October 1926, p.640.

22. Dinsdale T. Young, *Neglected People of the Bible* (London, Hodder & Stoughton, 1902), p.71.

SCRIPTURE INDEX

Certainties of CHRIST'S SECOND COMING

by J. Oswald Sanders

The return of Jesus Christ to the earth is a certain fact clearly promised in Scripture. Although there are differing interpretations of some Bible passages, nevertheless many vital points remain beyond dispute.

This book is not concerned with speculation or sensationalism. Its aim is to outline the central biblical truths — not to satisfy our curiosity, but to encourage us to live holier lives and be more effective witnesses to the world.

k
Kingsway Publications